Theo Baart Tracy Metz Tjerk Ruimschotel

Atlas of change
Rearranging the Netherlands

Colophon

Atlas of change: Rearranging the Netherlands is
an initiative of Ideas on Paper and is published in
association with NAi Publishers.

Photography Theo Baart
Reportages and interviews Tracy Metz
Essay Tjerk Ruimschotel
Maps Must (The maps were made in relation to the
5e Nota Ruimtelijke Ordening (Fifth Report on
Spatial Planning in the Netherlands)
Design Typography & Other Serious Matters
Editing Caroline Gautier, Paula Vaandrager
English translation Andrew May
Printed by Veenman drukkers
Lithography Nauta en Haagen and Drukkerij SSN
Bound by De Haan

This publication was made possible with the support of
the Ministry of Housing, Spatial Planning and the
Environment (National Spatial Planning Agency of the
Netherlands). Additional financial support was provided
by the Ministry of Agriculture, Nature Management and
Fisheries, the Ministry of Transport, Public Works and
Water Management, and the De Gijselaar-Hintzen Fund.

Contents

Available in North, South and Central America
through D.A.P./Distributed Art Publishers Inc,
155 Sixth Avenue 2nd Floor, New York, NY 10013-1507,
T 212 6271999 F 212 6279484.

Available in the United Kingdom and Ireland
through Art Data, 12 Bell Industrial Estate,
50 Cunnington Street, London W4 5HB,
T 181 7471061 F 181 7422319.

Printed and bound in the Netherlands.

ISBN 90 5662 163 7

Foreword

The Netherlands is changing at a rapid pace. We are continually adding new places, with new functions, to the old familiar assortment of residential neighbourhoods, city parks, farms and pastures. Changes in our economy, income, leisure activities and population profile are reflected in the landscape. Protected nesting zones for geese, compensatory green, leisure parks, cultivated nature areas, buffer zones, dog toilets: the land is continually parcelled out in order to offer physical fulfilment to every wish. In order to be able to honour all these wishes we start stacking things: a ski slope appears on top of a landfill site, a canal flows in the guise of an aqueduct over a motorway, a dredging depot is covered with sealant foil and transformed into a nature area.

This mutability of the Netherlands is not new; in fact it has always prevailed. Without the capacity to conjure land from water – a never-ending process that requires painstaking and ever-vigilant maintenance – a large part of the country would not even exist. The difference with the past lies mainly in the rapid mutability, quantity and variety of the wishes. More and more, faster and faster. Even as the government is going through the process of decentralization, it attempts to draw the broad outline for the process with a series of reports and memoranda.

As the government, at the start of the new millennium, reflects on the future of physical space in the Netherlands, this **Atlas of change** takes a **tour d'horizon** through the transformations the country has undergone since post-war reconstruction and is still undergoing – for the end is not yet in sight. The Netherlands has been, and continues to be, rearranged.

Photographer Theo Baart portrays, in alphabetical order, the new landscapes through which we move. Based on policy documents and newspaper articles he has selected sixty concepts that signify the recent changes in the use of space in the Netherlands. The language-oriented character of spatial planning in this country of poets and dike wardens – or perhaps of copywriters and ground diggers – is unfathomable. The definition of a new typology is also an attempt to control and sometimes to sublimate and invoke it.

Journalist Tracy Metz interviews thirteen residents of the Netherlands and describes the way in which their lives are changing along with it. In their capacity as consumers of space, the Entrepreneur, the Automobile Commuter, the Bargemaster, the Historical Geographer, the IT Specialist and the Vinex Resident, among others, relate how they experience the changing Netherlands. In addition, six observers assess the managerial role of the government and the intertwining of factors that determines spatial planning. Urban planning expert Tjerk Ruimschotel places developments in spatial planning in an historic and a contemporary context and analyzes the government attempts to manage and direct this. More significant than quantitative use of space, he finds, is a qualitative planning, whereby some places are full and others empty, at times busy and at other times quiet.

Must reveals the Netherlands in three series of maps. The first shows the changes between 1960 and 2000; the second series consists of cross-sections under the themes of recreation, public access and the national 'metabolism', that is to say, the transport of materials.

The third series contains the 'mental maps' of three Dutch people, from which it emerges that our perceptions and experiences of our environment diverge from the objective cartographic reality.

There is an element of duplicity in our attitude toward the arrangement of the Netherlands. On the one hand we are worried about its being full – or, as the Minister for Housing, Spatial Planning and the Environment, Jan Pronk, prefers to term it, crowded – on the other hand growing prosperity has engendered an attitude of: 'We want it all and we want it now.' More and bigger houses, greenhouses and business zones, but also more nature areas for the Sunday afternoon stroll. A runway and roads and a high-speed train, but also silence and darkness. The need for direction is ever greater, but the readiness to accept the directives is ever diminishing.

This 'Atlas' is an inquiry into the Netherlands of today and tomorrow. What do we want, what are we creating and what do we think about it?

Reportages and interviews Tracy Metz

Tracy Metz

The Train Commuter

**double time / poppies on the platform /
layers of urban fabric / railway, canal, motorway,
high-voltage electricity pylons**

Centraal Station in Amsterdam For the last
ten years or so I've been shuttling with the 7.21
slow-train from Amsterdam Centraal through
the Green Heart to the Alexander Polder, north-
west of Rotterdam. There is plenty to see, a lot of
built-up areas but also a lot of open countryside,
and I've seen a lot change. Just outside the
station they have slipped the angled cube of an
indoor climbing wall right into the slit between
two tracks. To the right of the railway line I have
seen the green, oxidized copper bows of the New
Metropolis science and technology centre rise
from the water, and to the left I am able to follow
every stage of the proceedings on the banks of
the IJ river from the train. The interminable
demolition of the indestructible warehouses, the
expansion of the passengers' terminal with its
undulating glass roof, the little boats that would
eagerly assemble around the crane of the bungy-
jump and honk excitedly when the puppet-like
figures tumbled waterwards.

Distance is definitely more a matter of time
than kilometres for the train commuter. You
don't have to know how far it is, not even in
which direction you're travelling – except for
paying and getting there on time, and trying not
to get annoyed you don't have to do a thing. But
motorists also look at their watch more often
than at the mileage. On the **Périphérique** ring
road around Paris, the distance to the next exit
isn't indicated in kilometres, but in minutes.
For the interview with the 'Lord of the Manor'
included in this book, I took the train and train-
taxi to get to and from Klazienaveen-Noord in
northeast Drenthe, a journey that takes you just
as long as it would to get to New York.

Unlike the car, the train has the advantage of

9

double time: while you are in transit you can read, sleep and go to the WC (at least so long as it isn't out of order or occupied, or taken by a junkie).

Eventually, every traveller develops a kind of biological clock synchronized with his or her regular route. I don't even have to look properly, just steal a cursory glance from my newspaper or book, and I know where I am. And even if you pay less attention when you look out of the window as time goes on – usually taking in the view in short glimpses – every traveller has his or her favourite places. So do I.

Muiderpoort Frightening, dark rapists' passageways beneath, a handsome tower up above. A somewhat oddly situated station where the track splits.

Amstel Going round the bend before the station you can see the Stalinist architecture of the Rembrandt Tower, standing guard over Amsterdam. Then the first layer of urbanity falls away – the buildings thin out, it already becomes green – but the traveller knows that the second layer is approaching.

Duivendrecht Transfer machine from the first generation of beautiful floating NS Dutch Railways stations, a continuation of Schiphol with an old village attached to it. The planners even considered fencing in the station because there were only passengers who were changing trains, but nobody who was boarding or alighting. The inhabitants of Duivendrecht had to lobby hard with NS in order to have a staircase built on the Duivendrecht side as well as on the Bijlmer side.

Bijlmer Past the honeycomb flats of the 1960s. Telfort, ING, Europeesche, Gouden Gids. Atlas, Centerpoint. One last belch of metropolitan pretensions before the countryside begins. In the 1950s this was where the Green Heart started; the rural is being shifted ever further away. Not long ago you had a view of two beacons from the train or metro: the AMC

hospital and Ikea. Both of them have now disappeared behind a hedge of prime office buildings, the colossus of the ArenA stadium, and the new multiplex cinema. A reservoir of large-scale mishaps or a new urban centre?

Abcoude The first stop where everything is green when you look up from the newspaper. Everywhere in the countryside you see fewer and fewer cows and more and more horses, with a growing menagerie of exotica in between: ostriches, Heck cattle, hairy Scottish Galloway cows, hardy little Polish ponies. Just before Breukelen there is a meeting of infrastructural Titans. The Amsterdam-Rhine Canal and the railway run parallel, the motorway crosses above them at right angles, and there is also a line of high-voltage electricity pylons stringing its way across the pastures on a path with its own unfathomable logic. Here begin the great open spaces of the Green Heart.

Breukelen The section between Breukelen and Gouda is the loveliest part of the journey. Paulus Potter and Jongkind await you here, at least if you have survived the confrontation with the roadside architecture of the Chinese pagoda and the matching old Dutch windmill next to the station. The most quintessentially Dutch edifice on this trip stands astride a waterway: a little octagonal brick construction with a pyramidal roof of red tiles. Behind it there is a big tree, with some cows dotted decoratively around it. I have no idea what function it serves, but that actually makes it even more pleasurable. And I have been wondering for years how you can make a pointed roof with rectangular tiles.

We always stand still here for a little while before we are allowed to continue under the motorway. The remaining little patches of meadow alongside the track are teeming with rabbits; a little further on there are Lakervelder cattle grazing, so funny to look at, as if their heads and tails have been dipped in brown or black paint. Along the track there are myriad examples of the cryptic semiotics of the railways; boards with significant messages for the engine driver, such as 0.8. 13. 114. 22$\frac{6}{7}$. 109. From the train I look down at the motorway, tracking along the long string of brake lights and the welcoming warm-yellow glow of the petrol station to the right.

Woerden The station is nothing more than a momentary disruption of the view. A little further on a row of thick-trunked pollard willows leans at a precarious angle above the ditch. If the light catches the meadows at just the right angle, the thin line of water in the little hollows that used to be drainage ditches flashes silver – traces of the old land parcelling. Autumn: cows whose ear tags and bony backbones stick out just above the mist. Spring: irises, neon-yellow rapeseed, lilac, hawthorn, cygnets. For the passer-by one of the most noticeable changes is the new, shining black or green plastic now used to pack the round bales of hay; the farms themselves seem timeless. Until you see the tractor competing for room to manoeuvre with construction traffic on a strip of land between the railway and motorway.

Gouda Goverwelle When I started commuting on this route there was absolutely nothing at Gouda Goverwelle. Now it is a real stop; there are roads and new houses where people appa-rently live. In the early spring, poppies bloom between the tiles on the still unused section of the platform. As inevitably as housing estates spread out across the country, trains are getting longer. Then there won't be any more poppies on the platform.

Gouda 'Grozette grated cheese' stands there in illuminated letters on the facade of the business premises next to the track. A little further towards the edge of the city, the gigantic new headquarters of some company or other is almost finished. Just before the bridge there is a motor-cross circuit – I always think that I can smell the churned-up earth. Here and there, but not so often any more, there is wash flapping on a clothesline. More and more masts for mobile telecommunications.

Nieuwerkerk a/d IJssel My only experience of this place is from inside the train, but it is still one of the highlights of the journey because of the fascinating juxtaposition of infrastructure here: a roadway deep down below, an aqueduct above it, and the railway running perpendicular above the aqueduct. Along the railway towards Capelle Schollevaar there is a cemetery, where not long ago an expansion was inaugurated, perhaps festively.

Capelle Schollevaar Nothingness: single-family units, with nothing else, nothing remark-able, simply nothing. Or it must be that I have to pack my bag, because I have to alight at the next stop. The layers of activity around Rotterdam are already starting to thicken between here and Alexander. Carpetland, McDonald's – the city announces itself well in advance.

Rotterdam Alexander This is where I work, in one of the many efficient but characterless office buildings on the strip of land between the railway and the A20.

When the editorial office of the **NRC Handels-blad** newspaper moved here from the Westblaak, we were almost alone in this vacuous emptiness. There was a shopping centre already, the Oosterhof, with the standard assortment of shops. Now there is a whole variety of office buildings and a furniture palace and a carpark and the Alexandrium, where the local traders can advertise their presence in neon lights along the whole length of the building. Densification brings the inner city to the periphery; the parking paradise has become an irritated hornets' nest, even the heat and power plant has sprawled amazingly. But I don't find it any less vacuous.

From my office I can see the flickering pink neon arrows of the Burger King drive-in and the railway line, where the trains shunt backwards and forwards. What kind of view will I have ten years from now?

Monique Dekking

The Midweek break (34)

**complete leisure experience /
safe adventure / subtropical greenery**

There is a pig walking past the children's farm. Not an exotic little potbelly swine; just a strapping, healthy pink Dutch sow with flap-ears. A happy toddler walks up to it with not a jot of hesitation, and does what everyone would like to do: she gives its curly tail a vigorous twirl. The pig doesn't even bat an eye and carries on rummaging along the cycle path unruffled.

This weekend it is busy in De Kempervennen, the Center Parcs park in the Valkenswaard in Brabant. Almost all the little cottages that are not undergoing conversion have been rented, and it is a fight to lay claim to a green plastic stool in the subtropical swimming paradise. The formula for a bungalow park that the Catholic businessman Piet Derksen thought up with architect Bakema in 1968, originally under the name Sporthuis Centrum, or Sports House Centre, still works. The thirteen parks in five European countries play host to three million guests per year, who spend 13.5 million nights there, catered for by ten thousand employees.

Competition has gotten stiffer in those thirty years or more: not only are the Gran Dorados and the Sun Parks sprouting up left, right and centre, but moreover, the Dutch have the highest proportion of second houses in the whole of Europe. But Center Parcs knows how to tread the fine line between a product that has been recognized for years – 'we now have visitors who came here as children, then with their own children, and now with their grandchildren,' says public relations chief Monique Dekking – and the ever more stringent demands and often contradictory wishes of the holiday-maker. 'We want to offer the most complete leisure experience,' she adds.

It all started at the end of the 1960s, when Piet Derksen purchased a piece of land in the southern province of Limburg. He wanted to do something for 'the people' and decided to provide the families from the towns and cities with a little place in the midst of nature, with birds and trees – even if it was just for a short vacation. His parks had to cover a large area of eighty to a hundred hectares, of which at most 15 percent would be occupied by clusters of four to six linked 'cottages' – as they are now also known here in the Netherlands. Bakema came up with a design for the cottages that marketing manager Paul Geraeds says 'is as classic as the Coca Cola bottle', with a flat roof and a separate terrace. The little terraces are staggered, so that everyone has a green view ('nature') but not of each other – in the city you already have to put up with your neighbours the whole time.

Derksen soon thought up other novelties, such as the wave pool and the subtropical swimming paradise. He was also the one who introduced the Netherlands to the notion of 'the midweek break' involving a stay from Monday to Friday, which is most certainly beneficial for the occupancy rate of the cottages. In 1986 he ventured a step onto foreign soil with a park in England, and now eight of the thirteen parks are in England, France, Belgium and Germany.

The parks must at all costs look natural, Geraeds explains. The grounds must somehow look hilly – if there are no natural contours, then they are introduced. 'The greenery simply cannot look like a raked garden. So there are no poplars, but there are pine trees; no flowerbeds, but yellow flags and irises, and even stinging nettles along the waterside.' The annual investment in greenery is 20 million guilders.

The heart of every park is a big water feature, which is either laid out in a fanciful form or made over fancifully, for example if it was an existing gravel pit, as in Limburg. These days the Center Parcs concept of 'nature' does not just include the indigenous; the enterprise has its own biologist specialized in finding, digging up and transporting the tropical and subtropical trees that are a set feature in every park. A 'back-to-nature' feeling is also a recurring theme in the TV adverts for Center Parcs. Just like the subtle but clear suggestion that a midweek break is the solution for a perhaps flagging sex life.

Monique Dekking and I sit relaxing under a cupola of this subtropical greenery in the Market Dome, the centre of De Kempervennen, where the shops, restaurants and bowling alley (with a maritime theme) are grouped together. The centre was covered over a few years ago: the trees may be subtropical but the Dutch climate hasn't come that far yet, and turnover has increased considerably since it was covered over. Parrots are roost in the trees, and a crane is picking at a head of lettuce on a little island in the pond. A crane? 'We lease them from the Netherlands Parrot Shelter,' Monique explains in all seriousness. 'They are birds that, for example, have been confiscated at Schiphol Airport, because they were imported illegally. So they can't be sold either. This lease arrangement is their only chance to escape a hopeless existence in the Parrot Shelter.'

Pine trees and tropical greenery, pigs and cranes: we want ever more nature and ever more variety for our money. Center Parcs has seen people's demands increase in every way. Our whole pattern of leisure is evolving and broadening, says Monique Dekking. 'Market research, in-depth interviews and questionnaires for guests and non-guests have demonstrated that there are substantive paradoxes in what we want in our free time. We want to do something together, but we also want to be able to opt out and retreat. We want adventure, but it has to be safe. And we want to be able to be active, but also feel free to do nothing whatsoever.' Or, as Paul Geraeds puts it: 'Go on a survival course or explore a wreck in a diving suit in the morning, and put your shoes outside the door in the evening to have them polished.'

Two years ago these findings resulted in a huge investment programme involving hundreds of millions of guilders, in order to broaden the scope and the appeal of Center Parcs for every member of the family. Luxury, for example: cottages in every park were converted from eight-person to six- or four-person accommodations. Jan des Bouvrie was asked to design the interiors for one of the most expensive categories, the so-called 'style cottages', in order to attract the pre-families, the dinkies and groups of friends.

The 'VIP cottages' have also been upgraded with a Finnish sauna, Turkish steamroom and bedrooms with **en suite** bathrooms. Monique: 'Because what did we discover? Forty percent of our guests come without children! We hadn't imagined it either. These are the same people who go walking in Tuscany and mountain biking in Tibet.'

The restaurants and shops have been radically modernized and none of these are franchises; everything is managed internally. The same applies for the Action Company, the new activity programme introduced 18 months ago. You can choose between daring and exciting activities such as diving and snorkelling, climbing, abseiling and whizzing down a zipwire, roller-hockey and aerobics – a family sport these days, to judge from the reaching and stretching figures in the sports hall this afternoon. There is a sizeable lake behind the diving school, complete with a wreck – there has to be something to discover, after all. De Kempervennen was the first location in the Netherlands with a ski-slope, an original use for the mountains of sand left over after the lake had been dug. This has now been replaced with the Montana Snow Center, a covered ski and snowboard facility with a lift, ski jump and 'real' snow. Every park has its own special attraction, such as a golf course,

a riding school, a jungle or a 'Discovery Bay'.

An indispensable feature of every park is the subtropical swimming pool. Pool supervisor Martin is delighted with the recent renovation of the pool in De Kempervennen. He leads us past the waterslide, which has newly added light and sound effects inside the chute, as if you were hurtling through a sea of flames or through a volley of arrows. The theme also entails quasi-Egyptian antiquity with a touch of Aztec and a hint of Easter Island. The baby pool, the paddling pool and even the showers are 'decorated' with plaster rocks instead of white tiles. Martin does think it a shame that he had to give up a whirlpool and a corner of the wave pool in order to create more space for seating, but luckily the apple of his eye is still there: the theme pool, where real tropical, neon-coloured fish swim in between real coral in salt water. It takes five hours of upkeep a day, he says, and the seawater has to be delivered by tanker, but the result is really something.

Before we leave, Monique and I make one more little trip through the supermarket in the Market Dome. The displays strike a balance between functional shopping and fun shopping. There is a lot of convenience food, a separate counter for the 'dinner service', an attractive display with all kinds of olive oil, pre-mixed cocktails right next to the till. The environmentally friendly hearth logs of pressed wood chips are piled high. Monique laughs. For her, they are the symbol of the feeling that Center Parcs is some kind of national treasure. On the one hand that results in strong customer loyalty – 75 percent of respondents to the questionnaires indicate that they plan to return within the year – on the other hand, you are also subject to close scrutiny. In indignation a guest once wrote: 'You are not allowed to gather wood in the park, but the logs that you see burning in the open hearth in the TV commercial are clearly not the approved CP-logs!'

Hans Elerie

The Historical Geographer

regional identity / rural idyll / working landscape

A lovely spring breeze is blowing over the Hondsrug ridge — just chilly enough for a hint of goose pimples, but wafting the promise of fine times to come. And, less subtle, the stench of slurry that the farmers are spreading over the land below. A landscape at work, where tractors move like slow toys over the fields in the hazy afternoon light. What makes the Hunze land-scape so special, says historical geographer Hans Elerie, is the open space. Therefore that must be the starting-point for future develop-ments, in his opinion, for instance when the provincial authorities are looking for new uses for the area because traditional agriculture can no longer sustain itself on potato starch. 'I am afraid that when agriculture leaves, this area will be filled with timber production forests or even residential developments. First you must have a vision for the identity and the characteristics of the landscape, and only then can you decide what it is you are going to develop.'

Curious: along this cobblestone road over the Hondsrug, with the river landscape of the Drentse Aa on one side and the Hunzelaagte lowlands on the other, I feel that the benches face the wrong way. The people in charge of placing the benches compel us to look toward the picturesque village of Gieten, the direction that Elerie says the amateur painter would choose, even though the view happens to be blocked by a mound of stored corn under a black tarpaulin and a surfeit of used car tires. True painters, Elerie says, would look the other way, across the Hunzelaagte, and attempt to capture its sense of depth as it stretches far into the distance.

That is why he is so terribly vexed by that straight row of poplars halfway down the Hunze-laagte: there is that vulgar production timber. It breaks up the view and has nothing to do with the narrative and the origin of this landscape. Besides, the province of Drenthe is becoming way over-planted. 'If you consult the old travel journals you can read the complaints of travellers about the inhospitable moorland steppe that used to be here. Through human intervention Drenthe has become wooded and it keeps getting greener. For the provincial authorities all this greenery is a selling point for the recreation sector; every tree is sacred these days. What I find so regrettable is that it means you can no longer see the cohesion of this landscape. These days you hear more and more **talk** about identity, but you **see** less and less of it.'

From the bridge over the Hunze river you can, or rather could, really see the variety in the landscape: the river dunes in the foreground, the higher Hondsrug ridge in the background. Recently the Drenthe Water Authority establish-ed a plot of new nature, along with a meandering brook where there was none before. The trees are doing well and now block half the view. This 'ecological gardening' makes Elerie grumble. 'This kind of artificial little chunk of nature means you mask the unique geological forma-tions that give this area its very identity. There is a tendency to make all of the Netherlands a modern-day Arcadia of forests and greenery.'

The notion that you can establish 'new country estates' all over the Netherlands in accordance with the same ministerial guidelines fills him with revulsion. 'It is absurd to want the same thing in Limburg and in the Hunze. And then we can better forget all that talk about cultural identity as soon as possible.' As president of the Broad Consultation Group for Small Villages in Assen, Hans Elerie strives specifically to give village residents a real say in the future of their living environment. This is also true of

Annerveen-Spijkerboor, which we can see from the Hunze. 'Those people even made a beautiful book about the origins of their village and their farms. They know a great deal, they have out-spoken opinions and they have consciously chosen for this environment and its openness. You must ensure that this knowledge is put into practice if the area is redesigned.'

Homegrown regionality was suppressed for a long time, Elerie notes, but is now coming back to the forefront. 'But you see the "area-specific policy" invented a few years ago getting bogged down in red tape. Equality is pursued at all costs, even at the cost of regional interests.'

'The Drentse Aa has been growing organically ever since the Middle Ages. Ash tree and brook alternate. The Hunze is different – it is a designed landscape. When the river ceased to be the only form of transport, the villages were moved to the edge of the peat colonies for purely economic reasons. These are the processes that have shaped this part of the Netherlands. Policies can be based on the contrast between the rural idyll of the Drentse Aa and the func-tionality of the Hunze.'

That designers and policy makers should not disregard local input is once again demonstrated on the estate of the businessman Evers. He established a pinetum with samples of conifers and pines from all over the world. He created a nature reserve on a heath, his rhododendron cathedral. Most of the year it is a towering construction of finger-like green leaves, now a riotous jubilation of purple flowers. The bumble-bees are beside themselves; everything hums with their excitement. Stooping carefully we enter. For one long moment the world is reduced to this: dancing shards of sun on the springy branches, the light filtered by the leafy cupola and a velvety carpet of purple blossoms under-foot.

The bloom, like so much of beauty, may be fleeting – the experience is forever.

Hans Mommaas Recreation expert

'Recreation is now a leading factor in the physical planning of the Netherlands'

19

'Our living space is increasingly being partitioned into mono-functional enclaves – home, entertainment, fun-shopping – and we move between them in yet another enclosed, private space, namely the car. This is transforming the city, which now has multiple new centres on the periphery alongside the old inner city. In the United States, where most cities lacked a historical centre anyway, they call this a "donut city", with a hole in the middle.'

We travel more and more for our leisure and fun to large-scale attractions on the outskirts of the city, says Hans Mommaas, senior professor in recreation science at the Catholic University of Brabant in Tilburg.

Examples are legion: the celebrated visit to the furniture mall or Ikea on Easter Monday; partying at Claus' Party Centre in Hoofddorp; shopping at the Alexandrium mall, with an area of shop space equal to more than half the area of Rotterdam city centre; Showbizz City in Aalsmeer. Multiplex cinemas are popping up all over the place, waste dumps are given a new lease of life as a ski slope or, as at Zestienhoven, as a centre for art and culture. 'Now the questions are: Is this a problem? How can this process be managed? And which government department is responsible?'

The way in which we spend our free time is exerting more and more influence on physical planning and on the use of public space. More to the point, Mommaas says, leisure is a determining factor in physical planning: 'At one time public housing was an important vector in physical planning; now it's leisure.' The battle for our time is even more important than the battle for our money. We are living in what Mommaas calls the 'attention economy'. We no longer calculate distance in kilometres but in time – that is the product that is in short supply these days. Time is increasingly its own domain: the fourth dimension of physical planning.

The importance of free time is, remarkably enough, inversely related to its quantity. Work hours may be getting shorter in many fields of business, but most working people do not have any more free time. We do have more money – thriving economy, more double-income households – yet we have less leisure time. More women have entered the workforce, for many people with higher levels of education there is a growing discrepancy between official working hours and the work one does in the evening or over the weekend, and men are increasingly expected to help with household chores. 'You would think, therefore, that we would be less active in our free time, but the opposite is true: we do even more in less time, and alternate even more rapidly between more different activities too. Activities that take up a lot of time are in decline – reading, for example. But even as people are reading less, more books are being sold! "It's on my stack.".'

'There has been a real leisure industry in the United States and England for a long time and this is also now establishing a footing in the Netherlands. In the next five to ten years the European market will be completely restructured too, because the economy of leisure time is becoming ever more global. TimeWarner, Disney, the American company Premier Parks that acquired Walibi and converted into the umpteenth "Six Flags", are not just media concerns these days, but more like leisure emporia, with cable, Internet, shops, amusement parks and video arms. Sport events are no longer an isolated phenomenon, but have to be coupled with entertainment, at least with restaurants and shops. The "core business" is not simply sport, or recreation, or culture, but offering entire experiences.'

The leisure market is about the survival of the fittest – competition is unprecedentedly tough and it involves huge sums of money. And not just within one line of business, for example between amusement parks or between multiplexes, but also between different kinds of activities in different places. 'The Pieterpad long-distance walking route, the outlet mall, the museum, the sports centre: they all have more in common with one another than you might initially think. When they built the Bonnefanten and the Groninger Museums, the cities of Maastricht and Groningen discovered how seriously they compete for the culture tourist from the Randstad.'

'What's more, we no longer feel limited to the Netherlands. Centro Oberhausen in Germany is one of the top five attractions for the Dutch; for me it is also closer to Utrecht than Maastricht. Disneyland Paris attracts more Dutch visitors than the Dolfinarium in Harderwijk. And when the HSL high-speed railway line has been constructed, Paris will be closer in travel time than Groningen. And the art lover not only goes to Groningen and Maastricht but also to Bilbao to see the new Guggenheim. But I can also decide to do the garden this afternoon and surf the Internet tonight. In order to be able to closely track the whims of the consumer, more and more companies are looking for the means to follow or even predict their customers' preferences, as with the surveys that Center Parcs also conducts among non-visitors and electronic monitoring, for example in the form of the combined customer-loyalty and discount card offered by Albert Heijn supermarkets.'

This fickleness in choosing a leisure destination is made possible by mass mobility. Mommaas: 'The level of mobility in leisure time is increasing enormously – during the week primarily for sports activities and with huge peaks during the weekend. We spend almost as much time on the road during our free time as for the workday commute; even more, according to some estimates. For many people the word "tourist" still conjures up an image of day-trippers, with homemade sandwiches, but we

have all become tourists. Take, for example, the hordes of cultural tourists who "do" all the museums in Europe.'

The new patterns generated by leisure activities increasingly influence physical planning, he says. Conversely, physical planning is increasingly dependent on our purchasing power. 'Every public facility, whether it be the national forestry service, a sports association, the art world or the recreation sector, must generate much more income on its own. This means they are by definition more dependent on the market and hypes. The need to be responsive to this leads to a high degree of flexibility and instability.' There is more demand, more supply, more mobility and therefore a bigger scale. The new recreation sites are mainly being located on the edge of town. This, in a sense, is expanding the urban domain. 'People are not prepared to take the time to get to the city centre on Saturday evening, because parking is impossible and it might not be all that safe. What could be easier than going to a separate leisure complex in the suburbs, where you are guaranteed a place to park, where you know what is on offer, and where you can rely on getting home three hours later to relieve the babysitter.'

Amusement on the edge of town is, all things considered, easier to plan and this is turning it into the domain of the families and the parents who are out for an evening. The city centres appeal to another public, more the 'swinging singles' and the couples without children who can find their own entertainment. The city centres are being organized, planned and visualized not only to please customers out for entertainment but also to lure businesses and residents with high incomes back to the city. 'Cities see the upgrading of the inner city as a means of attracting "footloose" companies, especially in new sectors such as media, ICT and design. After the many years of migration to the outlying suburbs, which confronted the cities with high expenses and low incomes, the city councils now want to offer new groups of residents a pleasant living environment, including a lot of greenery and water. The city centres are the focus of integrated planning and are becoming recreational environments. One component of this is "museumization": asphalt has been replaced by quaint cobblestone streets, with historic streetlamps in front of renovated facades. A city does not build a new city hall for architecture-lovers, but in order to give the inner city new cachet and prestige so that it makes a lasting impression on companies, residents and visitors. For the marketing of the city and its competitive position compared with other cities, this soft infrastructure of image and ambiance is as important as hard infrastructure.'

The countryside is also striving to take advantage of the massive increase in interest in the leisure market and its burgeoning growth. As the traditional agricultural economy gets shakier, the rural Netherlands is looking for new economic engines, including tourism and recreation. 'East Groningen is being stuffed with forests as we speak, not just because these forests generate money from timber but also in the hope that people will come hiking in them. The countryside is being transformed from a productive landscape into a consumptive environment. In that respect it has a good deal in common with the old city centres. The countryside is becoming a leisure environment that you can visit in just the same way you go to a museum or to a film, or a place where you buy your holiday home, where you go to a recreation area on Sunday afternoon or book a week at a bungalow park. Alongside the potatoes and cows, farmers are dealing in campsites or excursions or traditional local produce for the tourist market.'

This trend is reflected in the **Belvedere Report**, a joint policy report by the Ministry of Education, Culture and Science, the Ministry of Agriculture, Nature Management and Fisheries, the Ministry of Housing, the Ministry of Spatial Planning and the Environment, and the Ministry of Transport, Public Works and Water Management. 'This too concerns the search for new and reliable economic support for the upkeep of monuments such as castles and forts and cultural-historical sites. Among the most important sources named in the report are recreation and tourism. Today the urban and the rural must be created, consciously created, because they no longer develop spontaneously.'

In fact, Mommaas posits, the entire structuring of the Netherlands is becoming a question of cultural politics. How do we want our landscape to look? What image do we want our cities to have? At the moment such questions are not asked. The model that we still apply maintains that there is a city centre, which is surrounded by a city, which is situated in a province. 'We have no governmental response to the fact that these city outskirts are touching one another. They are dynamic urban fields in which all sorts of things are happening, making the "old" governmental boundaries irrelevant.'

'We need a new framework for assessing the pros and cons, with a strong cultural-political component, in order to plan these things bearing in mind their interdependent and dynamic networks – so that the physical planning does not just run panting after the market. At the moment no layer of government that thinks in terms of border areas, outer edges – even though this is precisely where the new developments are taking place.'

'Right now each municipality is making its own plans. In contrast with the situation in the United States, the development of the urban periphery has not yet been to the detriment of the inner city – the value of property in the centre of Rotterdam has increased, the Stokstraat in Maastricht and the Kalverstraat in Amsterdam are some of the most expensive locations in the

Netherlands – but it has been to the detriment of the satellite municipalities. Take the axis Haarlem – Amsterdam – Diemen – Hilversum – Almere. There is going to be a multiplex in Diemen as well as in Almere and next to the Amsterdam ArenA, in a dead zone! All are being developed by different operators who are going to sit and wait out the first failure. As a government you can say, "So what, let them build." You might also consider what the consequences of our having two redundant multiplexes on our hands would be.'

'It is imperative that we start to have area-specific discussions about how we want to structure this region. Which developments do we wish to allow and which do we not? This should not be an abstract or non-committal debate; on the contrary it must be very concrete, preferably based on existing investment proposals, so that civilians can also express their wishes and propose alternatives. In this way you get a mix of cultural and political debates about physical planning in each area.' Jan Pronk, Minister of Housing, Spatial Planning and the Environment, cannot solve this on his own, according to Mommaas; the most important thing he can do is give new impetus to this debate. 'Actually this is a task for the provincial authorities; they, after all, play an important role in spatial planning when regional and land-use plans are drawn up. Some provinces have grasped this, for example the province of Gelderland, which recently drew up a radical plan for the Veluwe national park in consultation with all the bordering municipalities. Most provinces, however, pay too little attention to developments in and between the cities. It will no longer suffice to cling stubbornly to the city centre; we must acknowledge that these new networks exist and see to it that these lines are linked together.'

Mohammed abd-Alhamid

The Refugee (44)

khalaá / the virtual Sudan / much too green

'Too green,' Mohammed exclaims. 'It's much too green here.' He shakes his head in disbelief as he watches the Dutch landscape speeding past the window of the train. It is still all rather artificial for the former desert dweller: the luscious, glaringly green grass, the straight waterways, the towering trees that lose all their leaves in the winter. It takes him some getting used to.

We are on our way to Echt, a little village outside Roermond in Limburg, the southernmost province of the Netherlands. On the outskirts of Echt, just off the main road, is the centre for asylum seekers where the Sudanese journalist Mohammed abd-Alhamid spent the first six months of his stay in the Netherlands. He was happy when he came up for consideration for the ZZA scheme, known by the refugees as the 'Go-and-live-with-your-friends scheme', which meant that he would be away from the tense, heated atmosphere in the densely populated centre. He moved in with a fellow countryman in Amsterdam, but he still has to go to Echt and back every Tuesday to get a stamp. He cannot do this electronically; they want to see you in the flesh. So early in the morning, Mohammed – who has a pre-dated ticket that he received when he signed in last week – and I step into the train, to take the opportunity to look at the Dutch landscape through his eyes.

When Mohammed gets back to Amsterdam there will probably be another Sudanese country-man waiting for him, wanting to use the same open ticket to visit friends in Leeuwarden. And in Leeuwarden there is quite probably a third person waiting to use that very same ticket to visit The Hague in the evening. And just as Mohammed has to go to Echt on Tuesday,

Abdullah has to go to the east of the country on Wednesday, and on Thursday Aziz has to go to the north. And everyone knows the others' travel schemes, and thus every community of refugees has established its own mobility network. At least they take full advantage of the government-subsidised tickets.

Mohammed comes from the north of the Sudan. He was born on the banks of the Nile, close to the border with Egypt. 'There is a green ribbon along the banks of the river, from a hundred to a thousand metres wide. That is where life is. If you turn away from the river you go towards the desert, that is into the unknown, into nothingness.'

Mohammed still often feels the need for emptiness, space, known in Arabic as **khalaá**. It is hard to find in the Netherlands. 'I feel as if I'm being suffocated if I am cooped up in densely populated spaces the whole time. I once asked Michel, a Dutch friend: "How can all these people live without **khalaá**?" My notion of how a country ought to be is a mixture of filled-in areas and empty spaces. It shouldn't be so full everywhere.' Last winter he went walking in the Veluwe National Park with Michel. There was a sprinkling of snow; it was beautiful. Is the Veluwe a **khalaá**? 'Well… in the middle a little. But then there are roads and pathways and a museum. It is more like a suggestion of a **khalaá**.'

Travelling via Eindhoven and Roermond, and then by local bus, we reach our destination. It is warm in the asylum seekers' centre, warm and full. The queue leading to the little room where you have to sign in is short, but just a hint of someone pushing in is enough for a hot-tempered young man to grab under his jacket for – I think, everybody thinks – a weapon. In a moment you could cut the tension with a knife, but it ebbs just as quickly. When he has fulfilled his obligations, Mohammed wants to offer me a cup of tea or coffee, but with little success: there are only two cups in the canteen, and the man from Sierra Leone who looks after the machine doesn't know where they are.

Just as we want to set out on the return journey, that one bus in the hour has just gone, of course. We scrounge a lift to the station in Echt with an Angolan with a gold tooth and an enormous gold ring in the form of a lion's head. He has driven from Leeuwarden to visit his girlfriend in Echt. He does this frequently. '**C'est l'amour**!' he explains with arms wide, laughing heartily so that you can see his gold tooth flashing.

Before Mohammed was transferred to Echt he lived in the Refugee Reception Centre (RRC) in Zwolle. Nothing had prepared him for the complicated layout of the old Dutch city centres. 'At first I always took the same route through Zwolle from the RRC to the Aldi supermarket, because as soon as I deviated from the familiar route I would lose my way. The Sudanese here in the Netherlands have a saying: "Never follow a canal, it will only take you in circles!"' In Amsterdam he now knows how to get between the various places that he visits: his lodgings in the Pijp neighbourhood, the Internet café and the Institute for Social History, where he is researching the communist movement in the Sudan.

As a child he had already heard of the Netherlands because his mother regularly sent him to the shop for Dutch butter, **semen Hollandi**, and later for powdered milk. At school, the geography teacher said that people in Holland lived below sea level. 'If the Nile broke its banks, we would pile up the sandbags and keep watch all night. The danger would last for two or three weeks. I imagined the people in the Netherlands heaving sandbags day and night, all year round. Why do they go to all this trouble, I would wonder, why don't they just go and live somewhere else?'

The train travels along the Amsterdam-Rhine

Canal, where there is a busy to-and-fro of inland shipping. Mohammed notes, with a hint of envy: 'There is so much happening on the water here! When I was a child, a steamship would go by on the Nile once a fortnight, and that was a big event. If the Sudan had only half the number of ships that we now see sailing by then the civil war in my country would already be long over, and there would be trade and communication and some sense of mutual understanding.'

These days, communication with his country-folk and fellow refugees is mainly conducted via Internet. 'It's very strange to think that there is a great deal more political activity in cyberspace than on the ground in the Sudan,' Mohammed notes. There are newspapers that you cannot get hold of twenty kilometres outside Khartoum, but you can read them on the Internet every morning anywhere in the world. Do we think that we can change things there by sitting behind computers all over the world and conducting long-winded electronic discussions?' Mohammed says that people talk about the 'old' Sudan – before the Sudanese People's Liberation Army was established at the start of the 1990s and the civil war began – and the 'new' Sudan. 'Now there is a virtual Sudan as well. Here we are living in that virtual Sudan. It is the only place where I can meet my friends who have moved, or like myself are living in exile.'

The Vinex (36) Resident

first step on the property ladder /
prosaic advantages / eleven houses, sixteen cars

'If I didn't have any children, I'd never live here in a million years.' Heidi Tijburg knows that for certain. She and her husband Pim made the decision to move to the Leidschenveen Vinex site on purely rational grounds. 'We thought, "we've got to buy our first house now, because the prices are only going to go up even further." Plus we had an eight-month-old child and I was pregnant with the second. We were tired of house hunting, and the thought of a big reconstruction job to extend our own house was even more daunting. As far as that goes, new housing is easier, and this house does have a lot of space. But I don't really like newly constructed houses. Leidschenveen is just like Hoofddorp: it has no history.'

'Oh, it's true that there are more convenient aspects to it,' Heidi admits when we have settled down with a cup of coffee and a biscuit in her upstairs office. 'The day-care centre is within walking distance, and there are a lot of children in the neighbourhood. And I know that new housing is a good investment. My husband works in Alphen aan de Rijn, which is a twenty-minute drive. Indirectly that's a plus for me too, because he gets home earlier.' She shrugs her shoulders. 'They're prosaic pluses.' She does find one thing in particular that is a genuine improvement on living in the city: 'In Groningen and Amsterdam I never knew my neighbours; here people are open to contact. Everyone is new here and you are more aware of one another. We get along very well with the next-door neighbours, for instance.'

Pim is a biochemist and now market development manager for a pharmaceutical firm. Heidi has a job-share post for three days a week as head of care in a nursing home, but she definitely wants to go back to actual nursing for six months or so – a managerial position like hers is difficult to combine with small children. The Tijburg family lives in one of the first fifty houses in Leidschenveen: out of the eventual 7,000 houses, 500 have already been built and 1,800 are under construction. 'There were ten applications for each house. There isn't a lot else in this part of the Netherlands if you want a large house with a garden, is there? We also had to join in the lottery. We definitely wanted a corner house; that way you at least have a little bit of a view. There's a greenbelt that runs alongside here. When you see it you think, "Is that all there is to it?" But the greenbelt is a guarantee that we won't have neighbours opposite staring us right in the face.'

'It's still so barren here. Everything takes a lot longer than I had imagined. Than everyone had imagined. The grass was only sown two months ago. The trees were only planted after we'd been living here for a year. The first year there were no shops whatsoever. You had to drive twenty minutes for fresh bread, to Leidschendam or Zoetermeer. There's even a two-year waiting list for the day care centre! When everybody knows full well that these are the neighbourhoods most likely to have a lot of small children. Did no one think about these things beforehand?'

The Tijburg family has two cars parked out front; true, one of them is usually parked across the pavement. 'This block of four houses has four parking places and seven cars. The block next to us, with eleven houses, has ten parking places and sixteen cars. You can imagine the rows. Even if I weren't working I'd make sure I had a car. The car means freedom here. In the summer we get in the car and we go to the old part of Voorburg to take a walk, because around here there's nothing. Of course I'd rather have lived in Voorburg, but then I would have had to keep working. This way it's my own choice. We wanted to pay for the house from one income and also be able to keep two cars.'

'In my family we had a car until I was sixteen and then my parents got rid of it. I'm from Stadskanaal, where everything is within walking distance. If we went on a trip to Groningen or the zoo in Emmen during the autumn break then we would hop on the bus. My father lived there his whole life, my mother from the time she got married, ten kilometres from the village where she was born. She hated my living in a rented room when I went to university; the norm was that you stayed home until you married. She was from the generation that stopped working on the arrival of the firstborn. My sister still lives in Stadskanaal. I like it there myself: it's friend-lier, better laid out, safer for the children, and what's more, the houses are half the price. Pim wouldn't mind moving up north, but there is no work there.'

We get in the car and drive around the Vinex neighbourhood in progress. There are a lot of ruts and mud in streets that are actually just a little too narrow, certainly for all those lorries that come and go with new kitchens, new sofas, new gardens. Past the Albert Heijn supermarket in a sort of building hangar, past the so-called 'acoustic landscape' of man-made mounds that are supposed to shield the neighbourhood from the noise of the train and motorway. A tram connection and a railway station are supposed to be constructed here someday as well. A basket-ball court has been laid out for the youngsters and quaint wooden benches stand among the winding hills. No one's using them – yet.

At the entrance to the new housing estate we pass the billboard singing Leidschenveen's praises with the slogan 'Country living close to the city'. Heidi sniffs. 'It will probably be quite nice here in ten years. But I don't know if we'll still be living here then.'

Winy Maas MVRDV

'After the Delta Works
the next grand projet, please'

The future arrangement of the Netherlands, according to architect Winy Maas, co-founder of the Rotterdam firm MVRDV, will run along the following lines: › Shortage of space will lead to the restructuring of the country. › The Netherlands is really just a city and can be governed as such. › We can expect the government to take a stronger role, not only the state, but also the municipalities, which will realize that everyone benefits from a coordinated distribution of tasks.

'The Netherlands today is an archipelago of municipalities that all want the same thing. It is gradually dawning that the demands for open space are becoming too great. It is not necessary for each and every municipality to have its own expansion district; nor can every municipality solve its own internal problems with employment. Specialization by municipalities creates more coherence and a greater reciprocal commitment. For then you need one another and one another's facilities, and the incentive to work together is greater.'

'Taking Brabant as an example, let's agree that from now on Eindhoven will be "Brabant Downtown" and Den Bosch the city for shopping and carnivals. Brabant is in reality a city of 2.5 million residents. It is a city whose mainstay is its green identity, a result of its natural topography – but that greenbelt consists of snippets, none of which is larger than a thousand hectares. Brabant is advantageously positioned between three metropolitan areas: the Ruhr, the Randstad and the Brussels conurbation. These metropolitan areas are the regional engine that make it an attractive residential area. The Brabant provincial authorities now want to have "The Iron Rhine" railway line run through Eindhoven. That is very clever, because that way you avail yourself of a connection that has nothing to do with the Randstad; it runs between Belgium and Germany. Now that's network planning!'

'New media are creating another kind of city: the city of the interior. You can be a graphic designer in Auckland, New Zealand, and work on an assignment for the Netherlands. Globalization only makes the call for regional identification that much greater. France, for instance, keeps producing more **guides**, more **produits régionaux** and therefore more authenticity. I think the regional is gaining more significance in the Netherlands as well. Perhaps the north would establish a stronger regional identity by being emptied out, and Rotterdam a stronger identity by having three million residents concentrated there.'

'Large-scale entities also result in a stronger economy. We have to be able to compete in the larger market and that market is no longer the Netherlands – it is Europe. Functional differentiation is an enormously important economic tool for ensuring long-term survival. Economic equality has more or less been achieved in this welfare state, but there is no need to strive for equality of space. By not putting modern electricity-generating windmills throughout the country, but packing them into one giant windmill city in Friesland or in the North Sea instead, that region can specialize and differentiate itself. By not planting little woods all over the place but creating one large super-Veluwe instead, by not digging little reservoirs but having one large super-river, you create an imposing national park. You can have more environmental freedom by establishing two or three mega-business parks, instead of establishing little business parks with their usual environmental buffer zones everywhere. By not building little new residential neighbourhoods all over the place but one large metropolis, you can create a more urban culture.'

The greatest obstacle to attaining heroic scale in the Netherlands is the cultural climate itself, he says. 'We want to do everything well, to short-change no one, and so we too seldom dare to be selective in our planning. Isn't there something ridiculous in a big project like a new road having to be suddenly re-routed because two residents object? In order to have contrasts, or to create large green areas, we must dare to think and act on a large scale.'

A retro-strategy focused only on preservation will not suffice – he is convinced of that. 'It is rather weak to want to preserve wide open space purely for its own sake of it; that is strictly nostalgic and only makes sense in the short term. It is more interesting to employ agriculture or nature areas as instruments in the layout of the country. Where do we want the super-agricultural businesses? We'll get the wide, open spaces as a free bonus. I hope that the **Fifth Report on Spatial Planning** goes further than mere preservation, that it also accepts the Netherlands as a city of 15 million residents – only a few more than Cairo. This city has an energy park here, a centre of excellence there, a large forest, an industrial park. I hope this will lead to a number of **grands projets** that will rise above the municipal, provincial or regional level.'

To achieve this Maas argues for stronger orchestrating powers for the government. In his opinion there is too little discussion about what the government must control and what it must allow to happen. 'There are limited opportunities for the government to steer, ...unless you wait for disasters to happen.' His face brightens up. 'A flood helps: look at the Delta Works. Western society operates according to an apocalyptic beep system. Disaster prediction is a more refined mechanism. You can use anticipation of looming catastrophes to keep the Green Heart open, or the river floodplains. If you accept that river valleys should be strips 15 kilometres wide, not gullies a kilometre and a half wide, you can create a super-Loire. You excavate those floodplains, make nice hills from the sand, and on the resulting loreleis you can build towns.'

Winy Maas wonders whether it isn't possible to do something with the capital available in the Netherlands besides building increasingly expensive housing. His proposal: 'Buy up the Gelderland Valley and the Rotterdam port basins, so that you can mix housing construction with business enterprise and everyone can live overlooking the water.'

In order to be able to picture this new contrast-rich Netherlands we need spatial design that stimulates the imagination. It must be far-reaching, heroic and attractive. Maas once half-jokingly proposed putting 'sixty whitecoats' together in an office tower in The Hague to come up with that grand and compelling design. For Port City (a Rotterdam with three million residents), a Super-River, the Biggest Forest (a Veluwe free from all those fences), a Wind Energy Park (all new windmills in the Netherlands on one awe-inspiring mound, be it in Friesland or Groningen or offshore) the National Spatial Planning Agency has established the 'Design Studio' to generate ideas for the Netherlands of the future.

At the governmental level, Maas says, the coordination of inter-ministerial projects could be an important organizing phenomenon, more important than in current practice. This is why he approves of the Ministry of Housing, Spatial Planning and the Environment working together with the Ministry of Agriculture, Nature Management and Fisheries and the Ministry of Transport, Public Works and Water Management. 'The assessment of the performance of central government is still too fixed on the criterion of deregulation, in other words: how much the state palms off onto lower governmental entities. But these are all small, fairly low profile measures. National government must also concentrate on major developments that rekindle the heroic scale of post-war reconstruction. After the Delta Works, after the land consolidation, now, please, the next **grand projet** to which we can commit ourselves and with which we can identify.'

Martin Grim wanted to be a pilot with KLM
Royal Dutch Airlines, but when that failed he
went on to study computer science at the
University of Twente. He completed his degree
with a major in computer theory. For the last
three years he has been working as a system
architect and software developer for the
American company Lucent Technologies
('My first real job.').

He lives in Almere and is looking for a nice
girlfriend, because there are not so many around
in the IT world. This interview was not conducted
face-to-face ('f-2-f' in computerspeak), but by
e-mail.

Martin Grim

The IT specialist (30)

hype / coffee break /

telecommunications software

› Hello Martin. Are you a socially incompetent
nerd? ‹ Hey! I think not. I love conversation and
jokes, and I like to speak to people on the phone,
correspond by e-mail and visit people (or enter-
tain them here at home). However, I do hear
(from my friends) that I'm 'different': people
often need to get used to me. I'm not sure exactly
what they mean. Do you want me to find out?

› No need. Where are you from, where do you
live? ‹ Born in Slotermeer, raised in Osdorp. I
got this job after completing my studies in
Enschede, and now I live in Almere. It only takes
twenty minutes to get to the office in Huizen and
I could rent a fairly spacious but cheap house
without joining a waiting list. I've also just
bought a house here, but it is still being built.

› What does your house look like? Does the
computer stand pontifically in the middle of the
room, or is it hidden discreetly in a sideroom?
Or do you stretch back on the sofa with your
laptop on your lap? ‹ There isn't much furniture,
but what there is fairly smart. I don't have a

computer in my living room. Usually there is a big pile of newspapers on the floor that is still waiting to be gone through. And magazines of course. I don't have a TV (nothing good on anyway, so I read the paper).

The biggest bedroom is set up as a hobby space. There are two desks: one with the computer and one with a sewing machine (I still sometimes turn my hand to making kites, though I hardly ever get round to it these days). I use the computer at home less and less. On average I sit behind a screen for more than seven hours at work, so I don't always have the inclination to mess around on it at home. At the moment, the software that I use most at home is Girotel (tr. a programme for electronic banking over the Internet).

› Do you have a car? What kind is it? How far do you drive each year? ‹ I drive a 1988 Volvo 440. A bit of an old heap, but it still works fine. I drive about 30,000 km/year. A little less than half for work, the rest private. I try to go to work on my reclining bike a dozen times a year – it takes 45 minutes. Sadly a big section of my favourite route is now closed because the adjacent land is being built on.

› What does your work actually entail? Can you, in principle, work from anywhere on the planet? ‹ My work at Lucent involves designing and writing software for telecommunications equipment used by telecom providers like KPN, AT&T, SBC, Deutsche Telekom.

Lucent's headquarters are in New Jersey. I have never been there myself. The European headquarters are in Hilversum, and I hardly ever go there either. I have been to Tokyo a couple of times, and to Naperville, near Chicago. I was there for a few weeks not long ago to carry out tests. For the testing of this kind of system I have to be in a lab, with access to the hard-ware. I usually work at the office in Huizen, but Lucent has an intranet, so I can log in anywhere within the company and access my own e-mail, documents and software.

In my opinion there is too little face-to-face contact. We would be able to pinpoint and remedy more problems at an earlier stage if we were to have more f-2-f discussion. Now, with one group working in the Netherlands and one in the US, there is too much communication via e-mail and telephone, which is slow and tends to cause confusion.

They (management) offered me a job in the US. We would run our own little business unit within Lucent, and receive a stack of options. I turned down the offer. It suits me fine here in the Netherlands, with my family, friends, hobbies and good perks (lots of free days). I don't want to sacrifice that for a wing and a song. I now have 200 options. They are not worth very much yet, but they could be in the future.

› What impact do you think IT will have on society...? ‹ Much of the IT world runs on hype, exploited by movers and shakers. There are also a lot of people in IT who don't have the faintest idea what it's all about. They studied philosophy and suddenly become IT experts after a six-month course. That's impossible, of course: computer science takes five years of study at university level or four years at higher vocational level. A great deal of poor programming and advice is to blame on there being too many of the wrong kind of people with too little know-ledge in this sector.

› ... on our own lives, our friendships ... ‹ It is all about being quick, too quick. And people want everything: the skiing holiday and the trip to the Caribbean. Perhaps this sounds a bit old-fashioned (I drive a Volvo 440 after all), but I often think that there must be another way, for example paying more attention to social con-tacts. Our friendships are too easily set aside for relationships and careers. Our quality of life is extremely high, that's for sure. But then I don't understand why people still complain so much.

› ... on mobility ... ‹ I don't really have much

faith in teleworking. I would like to do it (one day a fortnight), so that I can get things finished without being disturbed, but I can't see it working as an alternative to commuting between home and work. I would miss the conversations / meetings / drinking coffee with colleagues at work. Mobility will most definitely become a big problem. I do sometimes wonder why people (including myself) don't live closer to their workplace. In my case that is because of financial considerations: in the Gooi region you pay more money for less space compared with here in Almere.

› What will your work involve in, say, a decade from now? Will it even exist in ten years' time? ‹ The work I do now will definitely continue to exist so long as people want new kinds of telecommunication equipment. I also get the impression that mobile telephony is becoming more important than the Internet. In ten years, perhaps even less, expectations are that nearly every phone call will be made on a mobile. I haven't got a mobile myself – I'm not such a bigwig.

More than 60 percent of my work currently involves actual 'creation', but in the future this is bound to change. A job without intensive computer use is out of the question for me. It is part of my life, and the way I make my money. I've now got a Palm Pilot, an electronic pocket diary. Obviously that's more than a little game; I could barely survive without it now. Nice and small, really handy (no more copying addresses from one agenda to another every year), expandable, tunable to your personal needs.

Albert Teuben

(44)
The Bargemaster

**brown water, blue water /
scheduled container service / island with wharf and
holiday homes / Dutch engineering expertise**

The wheelhouse of the Stella Maris looks just like a big brother to the endearing film hero ET, the way it jauntily sticks its head out above the cargo and peeps at the surroundings. When a bridge comes into view it ducks behind the three layers of containers the barge is carrying. At the bridges the boatman must not forget to pull in his head in time: the containers can pass underneath, but the wheelhouse would be smashed off with a thundering crash.

To bargemaster Albert Teuben and his wife Nel, the Stella Maris is home as well as business. The wheelhouse is Albert's office. The whole world is at his fingertips. He can make calls on his mobile phone, fax cargo manifests to the terminal, communicate with the lock- and bridge-keepers in the area, e-mail one brother in Thailand and another on an oilrig, and surf the Internet if he can find the patience. He can literally steer the 85-metre ship from his big leather swivel chair with his little finger, at least if Nel helps with mooring and casting off. This she always does with her coat on, rain or shine, because it's a special coat, with a built-in life-vest. She cannot swim, nor can she learn to: she's afraid of water.

This part of the inland waterway between Lemmer, on the IJsselmeer, and Delfzijl, on the Eems river, runs through the Frisian lakes. You can only tell it's a shipping lane by the buoys marking the channel and by the signs posted along the banks: bolts of lightning, for instance, warning of high-voltage pylons, and two arrows turned in towards each other indicating places where ships can turn. Otherwise we are enjoying the scenery just as much as the pleasure cruisers – perhaps even more, for in our elevated ET-wheelhouse we look down from ten metres onto water, reeds and pastures. And once, in fact, to our surprise, we see the tops of cars on the motorway, whizzing by under the aqueduct at Grouw.

A year and a half ago, with a couple of barge-operating colleagues, the Teuben family started a scheduled container service between Rotterdam and Veendam, a 55-hour round trip, using a 1970s boat that was not at all built for the purpose, but onto which the containers happen to fit exactly in three rows. 'Most of the time I sail to Veendam empty, like now, and return with paper, milk and potato products intended for export out of Rotterdam. It would of course be even better if there were freight that needed to be taken to Veendam too, but we haven't figured that out yet.'

This scheduled transport service turns out to be a gap in the market, and there are now six ships plying the route. 'We carry as much freight over water in one year as 25,000 lorries,' Teuben declares with pride. 'That's all traffic off the roads. And away from our big competitor – the railways!' Needless to say, barge operators don't care much for the planned Betuwe rail link.

Inland shipping of containers is a new and thriving branch of the Dutch transport industry. It may be much slower than transport by road or rail, but it is cheaper and reliable. Inland Barge operators are happy, because this means that the slump of a few years ago is a fast-fading memory. Cees de Vries, of the professional association De Schuttevaer outlines the developments: 'Up to now there were large ships with four or five hundred containers on board. Just then a domestic market emerges: short distances, small ships with 24, 26 or 32 containers. In roughly fifteen years this sector has grown from zero to forty percent of all container transport in and through the Netherlands, and even fifty percent of the hinterland transport to Germany from Rotterdam. And it's not over yet, because we're looking at 10- to 15-percent growth per year. The Bavaria brewery, for example, recently decided to deliver all export beer to the seaport by boat.'

'It so happens that I'm not transporting expensive items at the moment,' Teuben says with a gesture towards his load of steel containers, 'but you can put anything you want in these containers, be it computers or beer bottles.' He has noticed that clients do not care much about whether their shipment arrives a day earlier or later, as long as they can be sure it will be there at the appointed time. And the cargo is secure. 'You can drive off with a lorry just like that, but it wouldn't be easy to take a container off my boat without my noticing.' This new kind of inland shipping may keep freight off the roads, but it does involve new infrastructure: transhipment terminals. Fifteen years ago there were none; there are currently 21, and within a year De Vries expects there to be at least 30.

In the spring and summer it's always lively on the campsites and in the little holiday houses along the shipping channel. But then the leisure cruisers appear too. 'How can it be,' Teuben wonders aloud, 'that in a country like the Netherlands, where you more or less need a diploma to go to the toilet, every Tom, Dick and Harry can take to the water without a navigation permit? It's mainly the boat rental companies that are blocking it. Still I expect that in about ten years a navigation permit will be mandatory.'

In the Lemmer-Delfzijl channel, the professional sailors ('brown water') and pleasure cruisers ('blue water') get in each other's way more and more. The provincial authorities and the State Department of Roads and Waterways realised that something had to be done about the channel, for the sake of 'brown' as much as for 'blue' traffic. An initially open tender produced a conceptual master plan by landscape architect Paul van Beek, architect Ben Loerakker and urban planner Gert Urhahn.

Van Beek describes the Lemmer-Delfzijl water-way as 'one waterway, two landscapes'. There is a huge difference in character between the Friesland section and the Groningen section, if only because the Groningen section, including the Van Starkenborch canal and the Eems canal, was excavated much later. Moreover it flows between dikes with trees, which give it a much stronger presence in the landscape.'

It was already agreed that the waterway would have to be made nearly twice as deep and one and a half times wider. New, higher, fixed bridges had to be built so that the professional boats would not have to slow down. For water sports Van Beek et al. sought alternative routes, for example old sea-arms as the Damsterdiep and the Reitdiep, but also new, yet-to-be-dug bypasses with moveable bridges. 'With the soil we're digging from the channel we can create a number of attractive spots around the bridges and locks. Take the famous Oude Schouw restaurant. We can build an island there – actually a soil depot – with a wharf, a camp-site and new holiday houses. In Groningen there are permanent overnight moorings for the professional sailors, which you can use as the basis for creating a real port of call, with houses, new nature areas, a new village. We've been working on the design of dozens of bridges and large earth depots, and all of them inspired by the landscape, by the history and the current needs of professional shipping and water sports.'

His team, Paul van Beek says, is working in the Dutch tradition of the art of engineering. 'We draw inspiration from the surroundings. So we wanted to create something different for each of these two landscapes, but originating from the same vision and the same intention. Therefore we didn't design a whole range of different bridges; in fact we reduced the number of basic types to three. The recognizable design of the 30 bridges and locks along the

entire length of the waterway will allow you to experience it as a unified whole.'

Friesland wants to expand its water surface area; water is what keeps tourism afloat there, after all. And as is the case all over the Netherlands, water management is having a field day: nature development, water control, reservoir expansion. Paul van Beek wants to make use of the changes to the waterway to simultaneously address the problems with water storage.

'At present it is a congested, narrow waterway, with solid dam walls that throw back the wake from the boats and make it necessary to have those landing places for waterfowl and animals. Soon it will have softer banks with reeds and willows. Our design is a plea for the preservation or introduction of naturalistic environments on a much larger scale. By making the bridges simple in design you have money left over for that.'

This is a fantastic assignment for a landscape architect, says Paul van Beek with enthusiasm. 'Opportunities to work on the landscape on a large scale in the Netherlands are rare. These days it's only possible when the rivers overflow or when delta legislation is implemented, as after the Zeeland disaster of 1953. When you get together to shape a waterway like this you almost feel like God himself.'

Auke van der Woud Architecture historian

'The landscape is a mental archipelago'

Asked to name the most significant change in the Netherlands over the last fifty years, Auke van der Woud needs little time to reflect.

'The Netherlands is being much more thoroughly exploited, in every sense. Whether it be chickens and pigs, or mobility or tourism: there has been an unbelievable intensification in exploitation.' No wonder, he says, that when Dutch Minister of Housing, Spatial Planning and the Environment, Jan Pronk, asked his colleagues in the coalition cabinet to tally up all of their spatial requirements, it turned out that an expansion of the Netherlands equivalent to the area of the province of South Holland would be needed to accommodate their wishes. 'The interesting question now is how we are going to interlink all these wishes and needs. This calls for creativity on our part. The political machine must also work to unlock this creativity.'

As architecture historian at the Free University in Amsterdam and author of the much-discussed thesis **Het lege land. De ruimtelijke orde van Nederland 1798-1848 – The Empty Land. The spatial planning of the Netherlands, 1798-1848**, Van der Woud is well placed to compare the hectic present to the past. The inhabitants found it no less hectic back then, it seems. 'I have a text from 1849 in which someone complains that the Netherlands, with a population of three million, is becoming so terribly overpopulated. Congestion is a mental concept. If you are from the densely populated Jordaan neighbourhood in Amsterdam then you have an entirely different idea of what crowded is than when you live in Uithuizermeeden in the middle of nowhere. There are indeed limits to the level of congestion and speed we can handle, but these limits are always being stretched further. When the train had just been invented, people were convinced that the human body could not bear such high speeds, that it would make you ill.'

'There is currently no collective consciousness of where that boundary lies, in the way the housing shortage was public enemy number one for many years. No revolution is breaking out; there are no spontaneous strikes like those called to protest other worrying phenomena such as unprovoked violence. Politicians will frame the issue of increasing population density in the Netherlands in some manner, likely as "compact-ness". Slogans in physical planning have been one-dimensional thus far. Mobility as a concept is not sufficiently all encompassing. This is difficult, for sure, because the list of demands on spatial planning is so gigantic that it is now almost impossible to approach it in an integral way.'

'In the past there have been defining moments in the planning of the Netherlands that did not originate in the world of politics. The Plan Ooievaar (Stork Plan), the first to include the idea of linking the great rivers to nature develop-ment, was one instance. For organizations such as the State Department of Roads and Waterways this was a real eye-opener. Another moment was **Nederland Nu als Ontwerp – The Netherlands Now as Design**, a 1987 exhibition and a simultaneously published book. These shattered the illusion that we could sit back and relax because all objectives had been achieved and the Netherlands was complete. Until then we had been making ad hoc adjustments, but **The Netherlands Now as Design** demonstrated that we have to design the future, formulate an image of how the Netherlands should look in 2050.'

'At the moment such creativity comes more from designers than from politicians. On the one hand this makes sense – in our society the image is more powerful than the word, and a design is more evocative than a memorandum. On the other hand, a design can only be such a rich resource if it is based on a sound programme, and that is too often lacking right now. All these wishes are purely quantitative. When you hear politicians talk about the future it is mostly about specific problems, for example mobility. That is a very narrow discourse, not really vital, in my opinion.'

'The landscape is an expression of this greater complexity, in effect evidence of everything we in fact do want, and preferably close by so that we can quickly get back home in the evening. The Central Office of Statistics has calculated that as much land is now being used for roads and infrastructure as for housing construction. The agrarian area must fulfil functions not only for farmers but also for Society for the Protection of Birds, for our drinking water, and for hikers. Agriculture has declined but at the same time become much more intensive. We keep doing more with the same area of land, just as we keep on producing more and more milk from the same cow. Compression, squeezing out the very last drop – the Netherlands is good at this. The landscape is a mental archipelago that must serve an unending gamut of objectives.'

'Everyone is actively engaged in this intens- ification. On Vinex sites, for instance, there is relatively little public space but a great deal of private space. This private space is quickly marked off territorially, with fences and bicycle sheds. There is no collective urge to vacate space. Amazing, really, that while we all have an aversion to congestion every individual is doing his best to fill up our space even more. This is a relatively new phenomenon, born of mass prosperity and the growth of consumption since the war.'

'You used to get by with one set of silverware and furniture your whole life long, and three times in your life you got a new coat. Now, on the wings of a prosperous economy, the govern- ment tries to fulfil this entire Christmas list. Politicians have to deal with voters who want contradictory things, who are members of the Dutch Automobile Association as well as the Worldwide Fund for Nature.'

'The **Fifth Report on Spatial Planning** and the **Nota Belvédère** – **Belvedere Report**, about the role of cultural history, have made spatial planning a question of national concern long before their actual publication. This is something novel, but this has not given the government the support to say no to space-eating wishes. We keep piling things into our already overloaded shopping cart. This leaves two options: either you invest all your creativity in keeping the cart upright, or you wait until it collapses. I think it is our duty to also consider the question of how we are to go on, if things stop going so well economically. The discussion in the Netherlands at present primarily concerns the quantitative question of how we are to realize and arrange all our desires; it is not about the qualitative question of why the cart has to be so full.

45

Norbert Zonneveld

The Car Commuter (48)

backroads / corridor construction /
brake lights / rubberneckers' traffic jam

Seven o'clock in the morning. The engine of the company car, a comfortable dark blue Audi A6 1.9 tdi is ticking over, alongside a pretty 1930s brick house in a leafy district in Arnhem. Norbert Zonneveld is about to set out on his daily commute from his home in the province of Gelderland to his workplace in the heart of the province of North-Brabant. Zonneveld, who trained as a biologist, is managing director of Mirec, a company specialized in recycling electronic equipment located in an industrial zone on the outskirts of Eindhoven. As the crow flies, a distance of 60 kilometres; by road, 93 kilometres away. The journey never takes less than an hour and quarter, and it regularly takes a good one and three quarter hours.

He has been doing this for two and a half years now; he is starting to get used to it. 'I now drive about 55,000 kilometres per year. I wouldn't have dreamt of it before, but now I don't bat an eyelid.' It helps that his car, and cars in general, are equipped with more and more luxuries: climate control, cruise control, automatic transmission, hands-free mobile telephones, radio, cassette player, a CD-changer for six CD's in the boot. The inconvenience is now primarily outside, on the roads. 'In those two and a half years I have seen it getting perceptibly busier on the road. The Netherlands is booming it seems!'

We aren't even out of the street before I've asked the six-million-dollar question: why do you do this? The answer takes us way back: 'I was born in Surinam and came to the Netherlands with my parents. We moved around a lot within the Netherlands and then moved abroad again. As an adult I spent many years working abroad, with international development projects. We spent the last five years abroad in Indonesia. When we decided to return to the Netherlands in 1991 we felt it was important that our children, now aged 15 and 6 years old, felt that they belonged somewhere. I wanted to spare them the sense of rootlessness that I experienced as a child.'

The decision to go and live in Arnhem was a rational one: there are good facilities, it is an attractive living environment. 'My wife has her own company and can work from home. And it was likely that I would have to drive to work, no matter where we were living.' That turned out to be the case. Zonneveld's first job was in Zwolle, his current employer is in Eindhoven, but the company headquarters are about to move to Den Bosch – it might be closer to Arnhem, but thanks to the growth of the subsidiaries in Belgium and Germany his annual mileage is not likely to decrease.

At the start of the journey, on the outskirts of Arnhem, the car commuter passes a beautiful piece of nature: a typical Gelderland country estate with open, grassy meadows surrounded by large trees, spotted with cows and charming glades. We turn right and then we can see the A50 trunkroad in the distance. If the traffic is already at a standstill, Zonneveld makes an immediate left turn, taking the backroad through the woodlands to join the tailback seven kilometres further on. As we reach the border of Gelderland and the Betuwe region, the traffic starts to 'get sticky', as Zonneveld calls it, and that can last for the next twelve kilometres, until the Nijmegen exit. This annoyance is compensated by a majestic view across the Rhine. Later we drive along the Waal river and lastly the Maas river, the sign that we are driving into the province of Brabant. But first, immediately after the Rhine, we pass by a remarkable example of corridor construction along the motorway. 'It starts with a warehouse belonging to the Kruidvat chemists chain, reached via its

own viaduct, and then the companies pop up one by one right alongside the road. Two years ago there was still meadow on both sides of the road, but now it only survives to the left of the road. It isn't very attractive from the road, or looking out from the company buildings. And everyone who has to get there uses the motorway that is actually meant for through traffic. The Netherlands promotes itself as the country of distribution and logistics, but the road network is unsuitable and the political decision-making processes are extremely slow and inchoate. Clearly society is not as easy to control as we thought, because traffic congestion is getting worse. It takes years before the construction of roads gets under way, while the decision-making process depends on the political agenda then in vogue. I see it as a lack of vision.' On the hill close to Oss the attentive motorist can see the situation on the road ahead from the brake lights of the cars. If they are intense enough, this calculating commuter takes to the little backroads. Otherwise it can take a whole hour to reach the Den Bosch ringroad. 'Then I often pick an eye-catching car or a lorry in order to gauge my progress later on. If I don't see the chosen vehicle again, then I've won.' The motorway comes to an end close to Nuland, and then there is a long stretch with intersections, traffic lights and police cameras, through Rosmalen with its homely, rambling landscape of gentrified farms, car dealers, and the old convent that now serves as an asylum seekers' centre. 'I really look forward to this bit. Often you see the residents walking to the busstop more than a hundred metres further up. Seeing their faces and their colourful clothes offers a glimpse of another world. It adds a bit of variety and that cheers me up.'

At last we reach the Den Bosch ringroad. 'Always a mess.' Zonneveld doesn't see many accidents, but he often sees the consequence: traffic jams. 'A couple of months ago, four lorries were involved in a pile-up on the other side of the road. And what is the result on your side of the road? The traffic jam caused by rubberneckers. But I think that most of the jams are to blame on drivers who speed along as far as possible before taking their exit, and then have a problem getting across the motorway lanes to exit at the last minute.' Once we are past this hurdle, there is just one more left: the traffic joining the A2 close to Boxtel. Now it is plain sailing from the A2 to De Hurk industrial zone. The office is a no-nonsense prefabricated building, with a couple of striking bantams adding a touch of colour to the grounds. After a journey of – today at least – one and a half hours the work day can begin. 'During the week I usually work through until seven, then the traffic congestion has subsided. I don't mind driving in the evening, when the car is like a decompression chamber and I arrive home relaxed. It's much worse in the morning, because everyone is under pressure to be somewhere for an appointment.' On Fridays, Zonneveld has agreed with his family to leave the office early, so that the family can eat together at least once a week. Monday morning is also an exception. 'Then it is so busy on the roads that it makes absolutely no sense to leave before half past eight. I can take my little son to school and we can all eat breakfast together. Then commuting has a small upside for family life.'

John Rikken

The Business (48) Consultant

grey zones of physical planning /
new functions / ornamental paving and
tunnel greenhouses / concrete parking boxes

'Every business zone you establish here along the A2 would be full in no time. But we won't do that, you know, even though Brabant is one of the fastest growing regions in the Netherlands. Business people understand as well as anyone that there are places we must simply keep our hands off.' John Rikken, policy adviser with the Bureau for North-Brabant Chambers of Commerce, easily navigates the busy A2. Today, alongside this essential Brabant artery, an almost endless succession of business parks will pass before our eyes.

The Pettelaar Park, where his own office is located and where, despite its name, the only hint of greenery is the landing pad for helicopters. De Brand business park opened a year and a half ago and is already practically full. The meadows on the opposite side of the A2 near Den Bosch, which many business people want to see transformed into business districts as soon as possible. De Herven, where, for better or worse, behind the large offices, the cars are squeezed into a shantytown of concrete parking boxes. Or the business zone around Eindhoven Airport which is set to double in size. 'The hotels around here are full every night,' Rikken points out, 'and in the daytime they serve as conference centres. Unnoticed, they have taken over the function of the city centre as a venue for business meetings. Going to the inner city is obviously only for fun and relaxation, not for work – you can never get there anyhow.'

What are the locations that 'everyone' believes should be left well alone? Rikken points out some examples along the motorway: the valley of the River Dommel, the sand ridges between Tilburg and Den Bosch, the area near Vught where the large road cuts through the country estates and old farms. The valley of the Esch Stream must also remain untouched, but quid pro quo: 'Then we do want a concentration close to Den Bosch. I am hundred percent in favour of protecting the countryside from the exponential growth in business activity, but then you have to concentrate the economic activities in urban areas.'

Rikken turns into a little country road on the outskirts of the village of Esch – a telling example of the developments to be found in the grey zones of physical planning. 'Round the corner there is a family company that used to raise pigs, but is now involved in transport. Next door, their neighbour has started a nursery. You might say that it is at least green and earthy, but it is as intensive as any industry. And those tunnel greenhouses of mouldy canvas don't make the landscape any prettier either.'

'It's logical that people seek out other sources of income if the agrarian sector starts tottering. And being located just off the A2 is pretty practical, that's for sure.' But it looks more like a ribbon-like business strip than a rural area. 'If you want to prevent this happening there are two options. Either you say that the landscape must be protected at all costs, because we think it is beautiful as it is, or at least was until recently. Or you look for new functions that have sufficient economic wherewithal to simultaneously support caring for the environment. Take this poultry farmer to the east of Boxtel. He is about to move to a business park near Schijndel. What will happen with those sheds? Just look at the farm behind there, which has already switched from pig farming to construction materials. Is that the view we want to present along the A2? If the local council doesn't want that then it must be proactive and buy up those barns and sheds straight away.'

And then? 'Demolish them, for example. Or use them to house a company with a management agreement that safeguards and maintains the surroundings. The company can then subcontract that work to a farmer who is looking for new sources of income or to an organization such as the National Forestry Service. There are agreements like this with farmers, so why not with companies?' Rikken realizes that this would require a considerable mental about-turn. 'In the future,' he notes, 'the community will not only have to pay for things that it wants, but will also have to pay to prevent developments that it does not want. Quality of life costs money nowadays, that's all there is to it. In recent years the government has fortunately become more business-oriented, but it is still only able to hinder or prohibit. We must adopt a flexible planning framework within which the government can also encourage and promote things.'

It is nonsense to resist the impact of economic activity on the landscape, he believes. 'The Netherlands is indeed a cultural landscape that was and will be shaped by economic functions and considerations. In the long term the landscape moulds itself to the underlying economic function. New, more resilient and stronger functions supersede the weak or the outdated and create a new landscape – for example alongside that little road near Esch. This also means that the living and working patterns are changing radically. Our traditional notion of the country bumpkin – wearing clogs, going on shoots, speaking in strange dialects – in Brabant or anywhere else in the Netherlands, is pure fiction. Today's villagers are either urbanites who have moved to the country or locals who earn their living elsewhere. It's worth remembering that half the Randstad was built by construction workers from Brabant, and the farmers earn more from a ballet studio or nursery in a converted stable block than from the pigs or the potatoes.'

Eduard Bomhoff Economist

'Scarcity isn't a panacea, but it certainly helps'

'Just look at the Gouwe Canal, between Gouda and Alphen aan de Rijn. In days gone by there were slums along the canal; now there are luxury villas with a view across the water,' says Eduard Bomhoff, Professor of Economics at the Nijenrode School of Management and director of the NYFER Forum for Economic Research, an independent socio-economic research institute. 'A clear example of improvement without government intervention, and of the effect of scarcity. Scarcity isn't a panacea, but it certainly helps.'

Bomhoff is a champion of liberalizing planning regulations for citizens and municipal councils in the Netherlands. 'The government is too concerned with the details such as the number of houses per hectare,' he argues, 'when it should be concentrating on the larger picture and then applying its policies strictly and consistently. If the government fails to do this, then citizens will no longer perceive it as credible or trustworthy. Consider this example: there is an enormous warehouse belonging to the Schuitema distribution company on the A12 to the east of Woerden. There isn't a single tree to hide it from view; the company in fact wants to be visible from the road. Woerden municipal council granted planning permission, right in the middle of the Green Heart. Three kilometres further on there is a similar eyesore, a large industrial zone next to Reeuwijk with a billboard: 'Land available. Base your business in Reeuwijk.' So people drive past and think: 'How can there be land available here?' Wasn't development in the Green Heart forbidden? Yet nowadays housing construction is nowhere more intensive than here right now, because this is where everyone wants to live.'

'Let me give you another example: In Zoeterwoude there is a Heineken brewery on the Old Rhine between Utrecht and Leiden. It's been there a long time, but now a furniture mall has sprung up right alongside it. That's allowed, but the same council claims it is only permitted to build houses for the offspring of local residents. A kind of North Korea, you might say. Ordinary people will be up in arms when they see this. How can we take those ministers and their policies seriously? If they don't even apply planning permission regulations strictly and consistently in those few places where it is extremely visible, what are they like when it comes to places where it is less visible?' That is why Bomhoff, in association with his NYFER research institute, has published a controversial report about the Green Heart. The main thrust of this report is to allow the development of a couple of ugly sites and treat the beautiful areas with a great deal more respect.

NYFER unleashed the same refreshing set of questions in relation to the Voorne-Putte island, close to Rotterdam. The report **Geld uit de grond – Money from the Land** (1998) calculates that the area to the south of Rotterdam is nothing but a loss-making expenditure. With a different policy it would generate money. Bomhoff: 'At the moment there is a stream of government money flowing in: rent subsidies and benefits for the unemployed in Hoogvliet, establishing wetlands nature and recreation areas, subsidies for corn and sugar beet production, and other things that make no sense whatsoever. Subsidised agriculture is often not the most attractive. Personally, I find the non-subsidized shrubs grown by the nurseries in Boskoop a lot more attractive than a field of beet. Corn and sugar beet bear absolutely no relation to respect for the historical landscape. In addition, the subsidies for sugar beet production are huge, while the provincial authorities forbid the construction of any more villa-type neighbourhoods in the villages. Soon they will only grant planning permission for the needs of local residents. That would be absurd and ethically wrong.'

'Only twelve percent of the space in the Randstad is used by people or industry,' the economist notes, 'while more than half the space is used for agriculture.' His conclusion: 'You can go ahead and sacrifice a couple of fields of corn and sugar beet, and the cows will still have a lot more space than the humans. What we say is: would it be so crazy to offer a small percentage of the land to the highest bidder, no matter whether he wants to build villas or grow roses? I can tell you what will happen with the land: it will become private-sector housing, of course. That is not such a bad thing. The population mix will become more diverse, and that would make Voorne-Putte more attractive. In Enschede, one of the poorest cities in the Netherlands, the city council made the headlines with its plan to sell a number of plots to the highest bidder. It caused one heck of a furore. We don't do this at the moment, but why shouldn't we?'

In the report **Money from the Land**, NYFER also argued for the construction of luxurious pri-vate-sector housing on a large scale to the south of Rotterdam, in combination with the extension of the A4 motorway and the construction of a Tweede Maasvlakte
(a second industrial zone in the Maas Estuary), partly financed by the sale of these houses. In 1999, in the report **Grip op de grond – A Grip on the Land**, the institute called for a so-called 'land-use levy'. This means that when the land increases in value because of a change in use – for example because it is used for houses or offices, or even infrastructure, instead of for cows or sugar beet – part of the increase in value should go to the local council, i.e. the community. 'It is the decisions and investments of central government that lead to the increases in land value, but at the moment the State sees absolute-ly no return on this. Now it is only the former landowners who are left with a big bag of money. It would be fairer if the community were to share in these profits. You cannot blame the farmers of course; they are just biding their time in the hope that their land will be earmarked for housing in the government's upcoming **5e Nota Ruimtelijke**

Ordening – Fifth Report on Spatial Planning. 'It is the fault of the government itself for allowing a legislative loophole whereby profits are siphoned into the pockets of the landowners. The current redistribution of the money from the sale of land is inequitable and thus socially undesirable.'

Bomhoff says that the price of land for the construction of housing in the Netherlands is high, in fact too high, because too few houses are being built. 'The maths is easy: if you allocate more land for housing, then the price per square metre will drop. In addition, you will then get new neighbourhoods that in the future will be more attractive than what we are currently building at the Vinex locations. The government policy of high-density construction has been taken to the extreme.'

And what about the policy of the 'compact city', which was intended to maintain the dis-tinction between city and countryside?

'Seeing where the city stops and the country-side begins is something that fits in with the history of the Netherlands. I very much want our grandchildren to be able to recognize the landscapes of Jan van Goyen, even in the west of the Netherlands. I am convinced that this is possible, with a bit more legislative flexibility and the readiness to transfer more land from one use to another. But we aren't doing our grandchildren any favours with those forty houses per hectare, because then all you will see at the front of the houses is cars and rubbish bins. Twenty houses per hectare is enough for a neighbourhood with single-family dwellings. Recently I was visiting a new housing develop-ment in Drachten, in the province of Friesland, where seventeen houses per hectare was the norm. If you are from the Randstad, you would immediately think it was a posh neighbourhood! In the Randstad only millionaires
live on such broad streets.'

Cees Zwanenburg

(54)
The Businessman

**sophisticated logistical operations /
new distribution centre / local marketing /
pernickety regulations**

With a joyous tug on the wheel, Cees Zwanenburg takes a left into the grounds of the bunker. The German bunker for submarines next to the beach and the pier is one of IJmuiden's landmarks. And part of it belongs to him. For years the bunker has been in use as a storage and distribution depot for Vomar (VOordeelMARkt – Bargain Market), the supermarket chain, operating in the province of North Holland, that Zwanenburg established with his father 35 years ago.

'My grandpa had a dairy farm in Velserbroek. He had too much of everything: too much milk and too many sons. So he sent them to IJmuiden to sell the milk there.' Cees' father set up a grocery shop on the main street, a unit now occupied by a tired-looking clothes shop. In the intervening years Vomar has grown into a regional supermarket enterprise with 33 branches and a turnover of 600 million guilders. If Zwanenburg has his way there will be 40 branches in 2003, with a turnover of 800 million.

He is still loyal to his place of birth, as a businessman and a local resident. He and his family live in Uitgeest, where the sheep meander past the door every morning like commuters on their way to their pasture, and trek back in the evening. The Vomar supermarkets are located in the triangle between Den Helder – Almere – Noordwijk, with the A9 / N9 highway as a lifeline. The management style is also based on the philosophy of 'local marketing': 'We know our clients and they know us. Because we are from North Holland ourselves, we know that sushi sells like hot cakes in the Food Village at Schiphol Airport, in which we have a

50 percent interest; that it sells fairly well in Haarlem, and that it's not even worth trying in Den Helder. The further north you go in North Holland, the more traditional the eating habits.'

'That is not to say that there isn't a lot changing there too. When I lived above the grocery shop with my parents as a young boy, it was always macaroni on Wednesday, mince on Thursday, fish on Friday, an egg on Saturday. Nowadays I don't know whether I will be having Japanese, Mexican, Thai, Italian or bangers and mash this evening. My wife Astrid probably doesn't know either. She doesn't decide until she is actually in the shop. You can find all the ingredients in our shops. If you are a supermarket then you must be able to offer a varied assortment, because that is what your clients expect. There is no comparison between the amount of floorspace required for this and that available in my father's first grocery store.'

The ever loftier and more varied demands of the consumer make it increasingly necessary to have a sophisticated logistical operation. Vomar will soon be leaving the bunker, which is now only one of four depots, in order to concentrate everything in a new warehouse on a plot covering no less than 55,000 square metres in a business zone to the south of Alkmaar. 'A warehouse like this is more expensive but more efficient, and means that we will be able to react to social changes. Your logistical infrastructure must be able to cope with those changes without it incurring prohibitive additional costs.'

The company headquarters is also moving from the tall, narrow building on the quayside in IJmuiden, where the fishermen used to dry, mend and hang their nets. 'Yes, that is certainly painful,' says the jovial director, 'but I understand why the council would rather have port-related activities here. What's more, we generate an awful lot of traffic. We have eighteen lorries that are constantly rolling over the A9. They are always full. Previously there were about 150 lorry movements per shop: every newspaper, every variety of cheese, and every sack of potatoes was delivered individually by the manufacturers. Once the new distribution centre is up and running, all these products will be brought together in advance, and the lorries will deliver goods from twenty or thirty different suppliers. We no longer work according to a so-called "item-oriented" business model, but to a volume-oriented model. That means less traffic on the roads as well as in the residential neighbourhoods around the shops.'

In Zwanenburg's experience, the government's spatial planning policies sometimes have exactly the opposite effect to that intended. 'As a businessman you sometimes end up entangled in the complexity and slow pace of Dutch bureaucracy. In hindsight, the changes have been amazingly quick, but if you look to the future you think: "Get a move on!"'

'I think that the big planners – national and provincial government – think too much in terms of abstract structures and pay too little attention to the consumer. Take Velserbroek, for example. It has six thousand dwellings, and two similarly sized supermarkets, i.e. both too small, and they therefore both have an average selection as well as too few parking spots. But the client has become much wealthier, expects a larger assortment and jumps in the car to drive to the really big supermarket. These pernickety regulations only make it difficult for those smaller shops and are also the cause of even more traffic.'

Zwanenburg is convinced that this kind of shop on the urban periphery is the future of shopping in the Netherlands. 'They are enjoyable and efficient. Grocery shopping is something completely different to shopping in the old centres – that is recreation, enjoyable but not efficient. The task of the spatial planners is to allow these developments to take their own course – they are inevitable in any case – without their destroying the hearts of the old towns and cities.'

In order to safeguard locations for his own company, Zwanenburg started developing his own projects; he estimates that this task now takes up one third of his time. He realized that he had better not be dependent on the government 25 years ago, he explains, when a Vomar in Haarlem burnt to the ground. 'The mayor was at our side mourning the loss, but he couldn't do anything for us.'

'Now, then we will do it ourselves.' A few years ago the company bought a factory warehouse on the northeastern outskirts of Haarlem, demolished it, and built a supermarket on the site, along with 38 flats and rooftop parking. When that became too small he purchased the building opposite for four million guilders, now known, after a 17-million-guilder transformation, as Spaarneboog. Alongside a Vomar, the complex also accommodates residential units, an enormous adventure sports shop, a furniture store, a coffeeshop, a Kwantum wholesalers, a Leen Bakker, a recycling company, and even a rooftop climbing wall. Zwanenburg sees an empty plastic bag lying on the ground, sweeps it up while still talking, and throws it in the rubbish bin – all in a day's work for this hands-on businessman.

It would be easy to sell Vomar to Albert Heijn, or the Laurus concern, or a foreign competitor, says Zwanenburg. 'The reason I won't do it is all about contentment; not about money,' he says with a broad grin. 'Being part of the race, that is what it's all about.'

And shopping? Does he sometimes do it himself? 'Sometimes,' he responds diplomatically. 'But Astrid prefers it if I don't: I always come home with too much.'

Cor van Zadelhoff

The Realtor (62)

a single Randstad /
housing and recreation in the countryside /
polo ponies / carriages as advertising

His first job, in the early 1960s, was selling cattle feed. He visited all the farmers around the capital. Until he met an estate agent who asked him to help him, because Amsterdam city council had just given him the task of purchasing the land needed for the construction of the Bijlmermeer. 'Two weeks later I was sitting at the kitchen table with the same farmers, but now I had wads of money. And they were interested, I'll tell you!'

Cor van Zadelhoff, himself the son of a farmer from Ouderkerk aan de Amstel, has become one of the leading real estate experts in the Netherlands. His name stands proud on the twelve branches of DTZ Zadelhoff spread across the whole of the Netherlands, an organization that has gradually carved a niche the world over. Now he mostly works in an advisory capacity, with a preference for the bigger projects, such as Schiphol Airport, NS Vastgoed – the property arm of the Dutch Railways, and the Amsterdam ArenA stadium.

Schiphol and its surroundings offer an interesting example of the development of the Netherlands, which has often progressed in leaps and bounds. 'In the Haarlemmermeer, the polder in which the airport lies, we have simply skipped a whole chapter of the industrial revolution. That polder was pumped dry in the mid-19th century in order to protect Amsterdam and Leiden from flooding, and it was a matter of course that it was used as agricultural land. From an agricultural area it jumped straight into the (post-industrial) service society. Now it is Schiphol Airport and all those corporate headquarters in Hoofddorp that set the tone. But unlike the Bijlmermeer, the council then was not so smart about the way it acquired the land. First they changed the land-use allocation and only then went to negotiate with the farmers.'

He explains the importance of Schiphol's real estate strategy for the further development of the airport. 'The press recently revealed that Amsterdam city council is only prepared to cooperate with the privatization of Schiphol if the land becomes the property of the city council. The city then wants to lease it back to Schiphol.' Van Zadelhoff thinks that long-term leasing is a monstrosity, a terrible system, as well as a drawback for international investors. He is dead against it: 'Personally I wouldn't even want to be buried on leased land!'

Are large-scale developments on the city periphery, such as the ArenA, a threat for the inner city? No, says Van Zadelhoff, who was chairman of the ArenA's board of commissioners for eight years, they actually have a positive effect. 'The ArenA meant that Amsterdam could be one of the host cities for the Euro 2000 football championships. In addition, an enormous centre has grown up all around it for sport, entertainment and business activities. Cisco, Versatel, Telfort – all those megagiants are moving there. Alright, alright, we do have to put up with turf that stubbornly refuses to grow.' It costs quite a lot to replace the pitch's turf three times a year, he admits, but it is worth it: this means that there are so many more alternative uses – concerts by the Rolling Stones, for example – that those extra costs are compensated.

The environment from which Cor van Zadelhoff operates is as rural as his work is metropolitan. In Breukelen, on the banks of the River Vecht, lies the seventeenth-century country estate of Groenevecht, with the De Zadelhoff Livery Stables alongside. It is an Arcadian idyll where town and country merge into one. He holds office on a long table in his 'Praethuys', the former orangerie, where the

chauffeur, Jeffrey, kindles the fire in the open hearth against the spring chill. The decor naturally inspires the conversation to turn to what must be done about the countryside and the precious open space in the Netherlands.

Van Zadelhoff is not concerned that every square foot of the Netherlands will be built on, not even in the west. On the contrary. And not simply because he himself lives somewhere where it is difficult to harbour gloomy feelings about anything. 'But we do have to manage it in a structured way, from the top down. Otherwise every municipality will only be out for its own interests. It is ridiculous that Rotterdam and Utrecht and Amsterdam all go on missions overseas in order to attract companies to base offices there. Together they form a single Randstad, after all. Just look at London and New York, which are both bigger than the whole of the Randstad!'

'Turn the Randstad into a single city, naturally with four centres – Amsterdam, The Hague, Rotterdam and Utrecht – and ensure that they are easily accessible by public transport,' he argues. 'In the middle there will still be a rural area with a few cities, such as Leiden, but primarily villages. The farms that are still operating can stay, but the agricultural use will, to a large extent, be replaced by recreation and dwellings. That gives more people the opportunity to live in open space and in the middle of nature.'

'Housing and recreation are fantastic alternative uses for the economically troubled farming community. Agriculture Minister Laurens Jan Brinkhorst recently took a first step with the so-called "cubit-for-cubit" scheme, replacing pigsties with dwellings. That makes it possible for the farmers to close down their businesses without it costing the state too much money.'

'It is difficult to arrange this kind of thing on a local level, so central government must take the lead with this kind of planning. The fact that it doesn't succeed is its own fault. Via the provinces, it has sufficient say in land-use plans, but they are trampled on. Fortunately the Minister of Housing, Spatial Planning and the Environment, Jan Pronk, wants stricter control over this.'

'There's still so much polder between the cities,' he says with a sweeping gesture towards the undisturbed view across the River Vecht. 'It is not so bad that there are fewer farms, so long as we keep the space open. There really is still enough space for housing and recreation as well as a bit of agriculture. Agriculture is changing anyway: potatoes and onions are of lesser economic and visual interest than housing and recreation. What's more, the increasingly intensive agricultural methods mean that we are able to produce more on less land. Let's meet the farmers halfway and stimulate other activities. It is a good thing that there are so many people living in the countryside. It means we can allow more farms to revert to nature and have the farmers manage this themselves, which is cheaper than when the government has to finance it. Either an urbanite will come and live there, or a small-scale e-commerce company will establish itself there – these are all people who have a vested interest in keeping the environment green and attractive and have the money to back it up. Cows and sheep then become a sight for city people.'

He has given another use to the country estate himself, namely as a Public Relations and Conference Centre, in the countryside yet still right at the heart of the Randstad. Leaving his 'Praethuys' office quarters we enter an arche-typical Dutch cultural landscape, onto which a layer of modern comforts has been grafted. There is a lambing shed behind the apple orchard, where a good hundred lambs were born this spring. In the half-open wooden stall, i.e. a roof and three walls, this year's little calves can get used to the open air. There isn't a single piece of straw out of place on the concrete floor in the stables. The thickset Watusi cows from Burundi shine as if they were polished this morning; their smooth hides have the warm, reddish-brown hue of mahogany. The bull proudly bears its elegant and formidable horns – at least one metre long. There are no cattle in the sheds next to them, but carriages. Dozens of carriages and coaches, large and small, open and covered, two wheels and four, in every size and sort – shiny playthings, to be sure, but also business. Big companies such as KPN, Bijenkorf and Bols keep their 'own' carriages here, with the company name in colourful calligraphy on the doors. The carriages are taken out with a con-tractually agreed frequency as picturesque, mobile advertising. Every year Van Zadelhoff rides out with the director of the Bijenkorf in 'their' carriage, both of them dressed up in specially made coachman's livery, in the St. Nicholas Procession through Amsterdam.

The meadows to the rear of the country estate are surrounded with the white ribbon fencing that indicate the presence of horses. The horses that I just saw inside will soon have company. 'I recently bought a farm in Vreeland, where I want to breed and train polo ponies,' he says enthusiastically. 'It is a wonderful sport that is played far too rarely in the Netherlands. There are currently no facilities for polo here, though there is a great demand. That is because of our soil hydrology: from way back we have had ditches every thirty metres for drainage, and a polo pitch is 140 metres wide. That makes it a complicated matter to set up. In Vreeland I want to make polo accessible to a larger public, with the opportunity to take lessons and train on horses from my own stables. This will be another example of a farm serving an alternative purpose, which many people from the densely populated Randstad will enjoy. Would you like to me to send you an invitation for a polo game in Vreeland?'

Pieter van Geel Christian Democrat-Provincial Representative for Spatial Planning in Brabant

'We do not want to become
the trashcan of the Netherlands'

All those catchphrases, concepts and little ideas that tumble over each other in the world of spatial planning are just like liquorice all-sorts, says the Brabant administrator Pieter van Geel: what seems like an enormous variety is essentially a great deal of the same. 'From the **Second** through to the **Fifth Report on Spatial Planning** we have been holding discussions again and again about decentralization on the one hand, and concentration on the other. But there is never a choice; it always comes down to a little bit of both. First we created growth cores, then nodes as a reaction to this, and now network cities are back in. The only difference then was that we first built the houses and only then established the infrastructure; now we are bit more sensible about how we tackle this.'

The real problem with the physical and spatial organization of the Netherlands is its management. 'We are no longer able to make collective decision-making work! The intellectual wherewithal of the administrative apparatus, the role of the various social partners, the role of the various layers of government – that is where we must direct the strengths of the planning profession in the Netherlands, not in modish concepts.'

A lot depends on whether it will be possible to turn the Randstad into a unified metropolitan area, a 'Delta Metropolis' that is attractive to both poor and rich and that can hold its own in the European context. 'Then you don't need to transplant facilities to the north, or allow Brabant to overheat. But then you must have a sound policy for the large cities in order to be able to tackle the poverty and unemployment on the southern edge of the Randstad, namely around Rotterdam. That is in everyone's interests, otherwise the people and companies who are faring well will leave the Randstad for the Zandstad – Brabant – and the weaklings will be left behind. Brabant doesn't want this at all. We already have so many people and pigs and

transport axes. It is also conceivable that Rotterdam will flourish, that the living environment will improve, and then everything that consumes space and endangers the environment wil get shoved to the south. We want that even less.'

'In the 1950s it was already forecast that the focus of growth between Rotterdam and the port of Antwerp would be in West Brabant. It took a while, but thanks to increasing mobility it is now at hand. 'It is getting busier. Brabant is obviously an attractive environment to establish a business. But we do not want to become the trashcan of the Netherlands.'

Is this the new Brabant apartheid?

'We already have our hands full accommodating our own dynamism. We have the fastest-growing population – we earmark an area equivalent to a thousand football pitches for residential sites every year – the fastest-growing granting of planning permission for business zones – amounting to 500 football fields every year – and we also convert the equivalent of a thousand football pitches from agriculture use into protected nature areas every year. The use of space per person doubles every generation, even in this province, where there are a great many people as well as a scattered spatial structure of villages spread across the arid sandy land.'

So you see spatial planning policy primarily as protection from the outside world?

'It is not our intention to build a fence around Brabant. But neither do you need to encourage that overflow by deliberately planning too many residential sites and too much business activity, or by failing to implement sound urban policies in the Randstad or construct a light rail system. Nobody wants to believe that I am so altruistic, but the interests of Brabant and the country as a whole complement each other perfectly.'

That is why Van Geel also gets annoyed about what he regards as the high-handed attitude of central government. 'That the people in The

Hague come and tell us that central government considers itself the guardian of our beautiful areas, the "pearls", because the provinces don't look after their patrimony properly. Central government should mind its own business; we'll do it ourselves and I really don't need any **Fifth Report** "pearl" designation. We are not just there to make a mess, but also to protect things.'

Van Geel, on the contrary, sees the provincial authorities playing a more significant role in spatial and physical planning. 'The central government makes the plans and the framework of criteria for assessment, and for the rest, in this decentralized system, the provincial executive is completely dependent on how that works out. The carry-over into day-to-day practice leaves a lot to be desired. Look at Brabant: in 1992 we agreed on a regional plan, but after eight years that policy only carries over into little more than half of the municipal land-use plans. Furthermore, we are not in a position to enforce what we have agreed. I am pleased that Pronk now wants to delegate this responsibility for implementation and enforcement to the provinces, because spatial planning regulations still most resemble those of a gentleman's club.'

Do those reports actually serve any purpose or make any sense?

'Sure they do. Thanks to the tradition of spatial planning in the Netherlands – the value of which you can only appreciate if you see how it is elsewhere – we have come a very long way in terms of the protection of values and structures. What are all the places that are named UNESCO World Heritage Sites? The interventions of the Dutch in their own environment: the polders, the dikes, the Northeast Polder, the Wieringermeer lake. The **Fourth Report** has done its part to ensure that the whole of nature has a place in spatial and physical planning, and that includes our regional plan too. Now you see that our dealings with water and cultural history as

organizing principles have become part of our national consciousness.'

Of course the challenge for the future of Brabant entails more, according to Pieter van Geel, than simply keeping the barbarians from the gate. 'From an historical perspective the use of space for urban activities keeps increasing. This is clearly continuing, despite all the limitations, and it has been doubling every generation since 1860. Our concern is that the rate of urbanization will double once again in this generation, and that the "light dusting" of buildings and housing that currently covers Brabant, will turn to "heavy snow" and everything will sprawl together. This province has 2.3 million residents, 6 million pigs, and 5,000 square kilometres of developed land, of which you see surprisingly little because we still manage to camouflage it. Pronk tends to want to circumscribe the towns and villages in thick red pen; I see more in the staking out of strictly robust greenbelts.'

'Brabant cannot be allowed to fall victim to its own success and growth. The quality of life and the social climate are in fact among our strongest characteristics. If we fritter that away, we are nothing. In this respect we have far too little regard for our cultural roots. The folk of Brabant have always been adept at adapting; it is something we have always done out of self-preservation. This results in amazing growth and prosperity, but sometimes also results in the loss of uniqueness and awareness of your own patrimony. We should think about this more, we administrators included. Practically all public officials are focused on growth – I sometimes think this is the criterion they must satisfy in order to be selected for a posting. I have yet to meet the first mayor who says: "Thanks, Mr. van Geel, but I don't need that business park.'

Frank Klement

The Lord of the Manor

multifunctional estate /
relentlessly straight ditches and roadways /
reforestation / lake-marshes

Everything in this landscape is straight as a die: straight roads stretching into the distance, straight rows of trees, interminable straight ditches that the locals here in East-Drenthe call 'wijken' or 'beats', rectilinear straight-edged plots where the peat was cut last century. After the peat came the potatoes, beet and cereals, which for more than a century was the basis of the Klazienaveen & Co. Ltd. arable farming business owned by Willem Albert Scholten and his descendants. In an age when you could still become immensely wealthy from the production of potato starch, farmer Scholten had a chain of ten processing plants, as far away as the Ukraine. Covering some one thousand hectares, this was one of the five biggest farms in the Netherlands and the biggest in the former peat colonies.

And now? Bulk products are not worth a great deal any more, expansion is impossible, the competition from eastern Europe is stiff, and the government is now intent on establishing an ecological 'bridge' zone here. There are nature reserves on either side of the estate: the Oosterbos forest to the west and the National Peat Park to the east. If farming has any future here, it is under glass; if it was up to the provincial authorities, the whole area would be another Westland, the intensive marketing gardening area between The Hague and Rotterdam, with its acres of greenhouses.

In 1996, Klazienaveen & Co. Ltd. decided to change direction: the formerly monofunctional arable farm is now being transformed into a multifunctional estate known as Scholtenszathe. The project is being managed by the 40-year-old estate manager Frank Klement. He has his own consultancy firm, Eelerwoude Engineering Bureau in Rijssen, Overijssel, and he spends two days per week as interim landlord for the company here in Drenthe. Though he was raised in the Veluwe, his father's family comes from this region.

Surprisingly enough, the farm has never had a farmstead or other headquarters, so he has set up his office in a wooden hut next to the potato silo in Klazienaveen-Noord. When we met there he explained that it is not so easy to become an estate; these days it is subject to all kinds of rules and regulations – at least if you want to be eligible for the tax breaks offered by the Natuurschoonwet, or Nature Protection Law – a law to protect natural heritage and prevent the break-up of country estates. Klement: 'We spent the first year struggling through the stacks of paperwork about subsidies and statutory regulations.' That is understandable once you see all the entities that have a say concerning the infant Scholtenszathe: the Ministry of Agriculture, Nature Management and Fisheries, the Province of Drenthe, Emmen municipal council, the Dollard Zijlvest Water Board, and the Face foundation, which strives to enforce the reduction of carbon dioxide emissions. Nowadays an estate is also something that can be 'founded' – witness the bronze plaque that was affixed to a granite boulder opposite the Veenkerk in Klazienaveen-Noord on November 27, 1998. And what would a multifunctional estate be without its own homepage on the Internet – www.scholtenszathe.nl?

The design created for Scholtenszathe in accordance with the stipulations of the Nature Protection Law hangs in Klement's shed. 'Instead of purely arable land use there will be a mixture of old and new functions,' he explains. 'At least half the estate, 560 hectares, will still be used for traditional agriculture. There will also be 40 hectares for organic arable production. The law also prescribes the reforestation of at least thirty percent of the arable area. We are planting 300 hectares with local tree varieties such as Scots' pine, alder, oak, beech and birch. Other stipulations are intended to reintroduce a sense of the small-scale in this extremely open landscape: trees must be planted along the 'beats' and the traditional arable land must be subdivided into parcels of a maximum of 20 hectares. In order to define these plots we are using trees and shrubs that stood here before arable farming began, for example hawthorn, hazel and Drents krentenboompje (juneberry).'

We set out on a tour. We drive past straight ditches and roadways towards the new forest: a multitude of scrawny saplings, with an empty strip of land in the middle, which will one day be a wide, leaf-shaded avenue. One and a half million trees and shrubs have already been planted here, and 1400 of the 2000 avenue trues have already been planted, but the spire of the Veenkerk is still visible from all around. What a labour of Sisyphus! 'Give them time,' is Klement's response to the scepticism of the outsider. 'In six months they've already grown half as tall again!'

Entirely unheard of in the era of arable farming was the concept of 'plas-dras', or 'lake-marshes', places where the water is allowed to rise again in order to create a marshy environment for plants and wildlife. Klement points to a strip a hundred metres across running alongside the protected Oosterbos peat moor area. 'On an area covering a total of fifty hectares we are allowing the water level to rise by more than one metre. This creates a buffer zone between the nature area and the cultivated ground, and will stop the drying out of the Oosterbos.'

The residents of the detached brick houses along the Scholten Canal all work for the company, or did in the past, and they have known each other and each other's families for generations. They were naturally concerned about their jobs when Klazienaveen & Co. Ltd.

started its metamorphosis. 'Nonetheless,' Klement notes, 'the new estate provides at least as many man hours of work as the arable farming company. There used to be ten employees and there still are. Forest maintenance, the forty hectares of organic crop cultivation, and the 'plas-dras' bordering the Oosterbos – there is plenty to be done.'

An important aspect of the newly founded estate is what is so attractively termed a 'high-quality living environment'. Twenty-four villas will be constructed on a strip of land between the two housing clusters of the pocket-sized village of Klazienaveen-Noord, with an asking price of no less than two million guilders. Is there a demand? Once again, the fresh-as-daisies lord of the manor does not allow other people's scepticism to fluster him: 'I think so. Drenthe is very popular, especially with people from the cities. And the new housing is not just for people from outside the area – Klazienaveen-Noord itself will get eight to ten new houses.' And at long last there will be an estate headquarters, at the end of the axis running from the Scholtens Canal, with conference and hotel facilities and the office of Scholtenszathe.

We take a look at the freshly dug canal that runs along the west side of the estate, where the water level will be allowed to rise by more than one metre. 'It is relentlessly straight, isn't it?' Frank Klement muses. 'I wouldn't have objected if it had been allowed to meander just a little, it would have been more cheerful. Never mind – that's just how this landscape is.'

Ans Rouwhorst

The Old Lady (90)

**three addresses / first car in the street /
that woman from the bakery**

As soon as the traffic lights at the junction of Amsterdam's Apollolaan and Scheldestraat change to green, Ans Rouwhorst hurries the cars along with the practised flourishes of a traffic policewoman and the croaky voice of an old lady. 'Get going!' she yells at a driver before he has even had the chance to dawdle. You can't pull the wool over Mrs. Rouwhorst's eyes; she has been living here all her life, and she knows every set of traffic lights and every paving stone like the back of her hand.

For a long time, more than thirty years, she lived above the bakery in the Scheldestraat with her husband Ton, adjutant in the Amsterdam detective squad, and their three sons. She still goes there every day to do her shopping, even if it is just for a pint of milk, half a loaf of brown bread and cookies for her visitors, like today. Every Sunday morning at ten she goes to mass, at the church just round the corner. In ninety years Mrs. Rouwhorst has lived at only three different addresses, each within a few minutes' walking distance of the other.

Son Ruud (61): 'Having a father in the police force was quite something in those days. My parents were well-known figures in the neigh- bourhood. My father was an authority and that was how he behaved.' When he died in the mid-1970s, his widow had to leave the house in the Scheldestraat. Mother: 'The council wanted to offer me a flat in the Pijp. I haven't got any fancy ideas, but a working-class neighbourhood like the Pijp?'

At home, she has already laid out the photo albums. The small, brown album bound in leather is the most cherished. It contains the photos of her first big journey, with cheerful captions in

73

white ink in a curly old-fashioned hand. 'In 1937 we went on a few weeks' walking holiday to Austria with one of my husband's colleagues, with a tent that we had made ourselves. It was quite something for a woman to go hiking in those days.' Ruud leafs through the albums with us. By now he knows the story behind the photos better than his mother does: 'As a young-ster I spent hours looking at these photos. That journey was a big adventure for me, an exciting adventure comic strip.'

After the children were born, the family rented a holiday villa every summer with Uncle Theo and his wife, first in Wijk aan Zee and then for many years in Zandvoort. Now she goes to Inzell in southern Germany almost every year, staying with friends of Ruud and his wife.

Son: 'Now that Father has passed on, you hardly go anywhere else, do you?' Mother: 'It's different there, that's the nice thing.'

The family was always close, in every sense. 'Every evening around ten o'clock my brother-in-law Theo and his wife would come to visit,' Mrs. Rouwhorst explains. 'Then my husband and Theo would go and play billiards in the café on the corner, while we women stayed in and chatted, including my mother, who lived with us for more than 25 years.'

'On Sundays at about five o'clock we always had drinks, either at our house or my brother's house on the Europaplein.' Even after Ruud was married, the two generations still very much liked to go on holiday together. And he still picks up his mother every Wednesday for dinner – even though these days it often means a hour and a half's drive between the Haar-lemmerdijk and the Scheldebuurt.

Son: 'We had the first car in the Scheldestraat. It was a beige Volkswagen Beetle, which we nicknamed Bobbie. It was always parked in front of the house, totally alone in that wide street. We would sit in the bay window on the first floor looking at it. That must have been

in 1961 or '62. I went on honeymoon in it.'

'Uncle Theo had a car before we even had a telephone. First he had a black Ford, then a red Vanguard. On Sundays we would often go for a drive, to the recreation area in Apeldoorn, or to Zandvoort to look for a villa for the summer.'

The family is no longer through and through 'Amsterdams'. Ruud still lives in the city, having taken over Uncle Theo's home furnishings business on the Haarlemmerdijk and the apart-ment that comes with it. One of his brothers lives in Castricum and works in Amsterdam; the other lives in Lisse and often travels to Poland for the American company where he works.

While cars, air travel, country houses and holidays abroad are perfectly normal for this generation, Mrs. Rouwhorst's world is as large, or as small, as it always was. A year and a half ago she did add a new stop to her daily tour: at lunchtime she goes to the Oude Rai retirement home for a hot meal.

On the way there we review the neighbourhood. A great deal has changed, Mrs. Rouwhorst is sure of that. But as we look at them one by one, it turns out that most of the businesses and shops have remained the same, with different owners of course. The pharmacy, the butcher, the grocer, the bike shop, the tobacconist, the florist, the shop for household goods – they are still there. It's different nevertheless, she says, shabbier. 'It used to be a respectable neighbourhood, the Rivierenbuurt, but now it's run down. The people are totally different, you see.' The Haarlemmerdijk, where Ruud's business is located, on the other hand, has become much more fashionable.

Does Mrs. Rouwhorst still know many people in the neighbourhood? 'They are all dead, or they've moved away. That's how it goes as you get older.' But not everyone from before has left: 'Ah, there's that woman from the bakery.'

Jan Pronk Minister of Housing, Spatial Planning and the Environment (Labour Party)

'As a civil servant you can better not place too much faith in the clout of capital'

Before you know it, says Jan Pronk, you're the minister for Spatial Adjustment instead of Spatial Planning. You get overtaken from left and right; your colleagues in The Hague – the Ministry for Economic Affairs, for example, and Transport, and Nature Management – all make their own plans and policy that impact the planning and layout of the Netherlands. It would therefore be sensible to reclassify the ministries. But to begin with, provincial executives and municipalities must counter the explosive growth in the acquisition of space through better, if need be mandatory, interdepartmental consultation about who develops what where. And residents themselves will have more say about their environment: 'They are the real experts.'

What do you see as the ideal Netherlands?
'Varied. Visitors from abroad find this man-made land of ours commendably arranged and surprisingly diverse. We must maintain this diversity, including the historical. You should be able to recognize the history in the present. It is part of our cultural baggage.'

'In Scheveningen, where I grew up, a lot has changed, and yet the structure has remained the same. Despite the many technological developments, the large infrastructural works and the considerable population growth we have managed to maintain the structure of the landscape and of the cities – from a macro point of view. This is also true for Rotterdam. The city architects, planners and spatial planners of the Netherlands obviously decided to build on what already existed.'

Can the government steer the process of change? You advocate state control, but the government has given up a great deal of power through deregulation and privatization – too much, in fact, according to the Scientific Council for Government Policy.
'I am not calling for control; I strive to be a director. That is what is expected of me. But the job of director in itself is not that, um,

far-reaching. The conductor tries to bring others into harmony, but he has not written the music and he does not perform it.'

'I would like to decentralize even more to provincial or local authorities. The concept of "spatial quality" is most relevant to people who live and work in a particular place. I do not want to control all this bureaucratically from The Hague. There must be counterbalance coming from the region, from residents' own living, housing, employment and recreational environments.'

'This is not always the way The Hague sees things, by any means. Almost every department has developed its own policy that has a bearing on land use. Countless sector reports have been published in the last several years: about the quality of the rural areas, the Multi-Year Plan for Infrastructure and Transport, about the land-use economy, about the regional airports, about the future of business sites, about Schiphol, about the future of the port of Rotterdam. You cannot put a stop to that. I have, however, tried to have all these reports follow the same preparatory process in decision-making, so that they all reflect approximately the same thinking. This should lead to the selection, and accommodation, and combination of such functions as nature management and recreation, and densification of the use of space for dwellings and business sites.'

When this second coalition cabinet, Paars II, came to power, we heard a great deal about 'corridors' that were to be developed. We haven't heard anything about them since, but there they are anyway.
'I'm against ribbon-like linear construction zones. A corridor as a combination of road, railway and waterway is fine, but it is not an concept for settlement or urbanization. Never! Instead I have come up with the development of the urban networks. The corridor may not be such a hot political item now, but in fact you constantly see buildings under construction

alongside the motorways. It is all the result of decisions taken two decades ago. And it is fairly disastrous, because the open space is literally split in two by that wide strip of roadway and buildings. This is difficult for me to stop, except by opposing it as a concept and by incorporating recommendations in the **Fifth Report on Spatial Planning** in the hope that these will be translated into the regional plans and planning permission guidelines.'

> You could argue that a high standard of living is bad for spatial planning. You can buy space, and as the standard of living goes up, awareness of the public interest goes down. Measures to limit and forbid are hardly popular.

'The Dutch are fairly reasonable when it comes to the planning of their country, because no citizen is solely a housing consumer, or solely an employee. Of course nobody is so reasonable the whole time – look at the high priority given to the automobile – so you do have to shepherd them in the right direction. You can do this by making them bear the costs themselves, for example through highway tolls, and by delegating a lot to the residential areas themselves, where people can discuss the planning of their village, region, city or province. When the decisions are only handed down from The Hague, they are too far removed from those citizens.'

> You want to delegate to the municipalities, among others, but they are one another's competitors. Every municipality wants to establish at least one more business zone and build at least one more residential neighbourhood.

'It is the job of the minister for spatial planning and of the provincial authorities to get municipalities to agree among themselves about the utilization of space. Competition for space always leads to excessive use of space, for example two separate business zones. In the **Fifth Report** we will designate – after consult-

ation – urban networks that will be obliged to enter into consultations about plans such as a new residential neighbourhood, hospital or recreation area. They will then have to reach agreement on where the best locations are and will be jointly responsible for the quality of the open space.'

'I think it would be a good idea for Amsterdam, Utrecht, The Hague and Rotterdam to look at what is good for the area as a whole, instead of each of them just expanding a little on their own.'

'Alongside the **Fifth Report** I am working on a revision of the Spatial Planning Act incorporating this obligation to cooperate. I want to establish a certain hierarchy of planning: the national spatial plan entails a global character on which the regional plans must be based. The local municipality's structural plans, or at least its planning permission decisions, will be aligned with these regional plans. I also want physical plans to be updated every ten years. In a number of municipalities there are things that are undesirable in this day and age, but were made possible by outdated physical planning. Municipalities that fail to do this could, for instance, lose the right to issue building permits. There is a great deal of opposition to this, but the alternative is to transfer control to The Hague. And the last thing I want is to give the impression that I am engaged in centralizing things.'

> Isn't that what you are actually doing anyway?

'Most certainly not! I want to make a number of broad decisions at the national level, for example about the Wadden Sea in Friesland, or the national parks. I also want it nationally decreed that areas be clearly demarcated – red around the cities, green around valuable landscapes – but I do not want to dictate where these demarcations are drawn. I want to give the four sectors of the country – north, south, east and west – more administrative authority to improve this quality.'

Sectors? Are you introducing a new layer of government in the Netherlands?

'No, these sectors are a fairly natural way of viewing the Netherlands in a larger context. I do not want to have to sit down at a table with twelve provinces. Above all, I would like the provinces to talk with each other about a broader vision for their sectors. We include the larger cities here.'

You asked your colleagues in the cabinet to calculate how much space they need over the next few years. The result, the 'Accounting for Space' report, showed that this would amount to an area the size of the province of South Holland. So the Netherlands is indeed full?

'Did I use the word full? I prefer to say crowded, because crowded is dynamic. The quality of space can also be defined in terms of how living feels. It is alright if it's crowded, as long as it's quiet somewhere else. And as long as you can go from the crowded to the quiet. It is vital for people, and especially in the west, that there are accessible areas where it is quiet, dark, open or green.'

'The west of the country cannot accommodate all the housing and employment needs, so you will have to transfer something elsewhere in the Netherlands, in accordance with local wishes. Not like in the 1970s with a policy of dispersed development, but by leading, i.e. through the decisions that you make about where you construct infrastructure and housing. Perhaps we will, after all, urbanize a number of areas that we have considered buffer zones thus far. But then you must draw clear boundaries around what you genuinely want to preserve. And densify a great deal. I support urbanization in areas where space has already been appropriated, or planning permission granted, but not an endless succession of new suburbs. You can achieve high-quality results on a small surface area; we managed this in the cities in the past. Only wanting green and broad and flat and low-rise

and a car out front is one-sided. I wonder whether everyone really wants that. And whether those who do want it, only want it because they don't know anything else.'

You want a different classification of the ministries?

'I'm increasingly in favour of calling this the Ministry for Living, Space and the Environment. But in fact the whole subdivision and organization of government departments is no longer adequate. The administrative function would be more meaningful if physical and spatial planning and infrastructure fell under the purview of one minister. In the area of spatial planning as well as the environment you are always fighting fires as regards the hardware – the Ministry of Transport, Public Works and Water Management or the Ministry of Economic Affairs. We simply have too many ministries.'

'It is conceivable that we might opt for a more limited number of public conglomerates with a more integrated political accountability. I also think that the development of the Netherlands in a European context should be much more the responsibility of one party, because a great deal of the policy that you implement is input for your negotiating position in Brussels.'

To what extent is the Netherlands still concerned with its own planning, given the increasing integration of the Netherlands in Europe? This has a great deal of impact on the infrastructure and competitive position of the Netherlands.

'Who else would it concern? Even if the city of Aachen were to decide to make its land available for ten guilders a square metre less than the city of Maastricht, that would be a marginal phenomenon. I don't mind such competition that much either. If it means space is acquired elsewhere, fine. On a macro level we can permit ourselves a great deal: we are attractive; we do not have to hold companies by the hand and plead with them to set up shop here.'

'I think it important to have a number of infra-structural communications facilities with the rest of Europe, such as the HSL high-speed railway. That doesn't mean we that we cannot sometimes swim against the current. The HSL is needed; the HSL-East is conceivable but not imperative. The Zuiderzee line is needed within the Netherlands, but extending it through to Hamburg and Berlin is not urgent. We are getting a lot thrown at us from abroad, but we make the choices ourselves.'

When the 'New Map of the Netherlands' was published in 1997, for the first time combining all pending plans up to the year 2005, it also included optimistic calculations. The Netherlands does have the most residents per hectare in Europe, but only eight percent of it is built-up.

'Humbug. You can see that when you fly over a tropical rainforest. That whole cabbage patch looks completely different the moment there's a hole in it for agriculture or logging. The forest is no longer the coherent entity it used to be. You see the same thing in the Green Heart. It is very large, but because of the greenhouses and urbanization, even though they don't take up so many square metres, you've lost your open space. Either it's completely open or it isn't open.'

If you are so in favour of contrast and diversity in the landscape and so against 'littering', why did you allow the construction of superstores?
'We are against isolated stores in the middle of open fields, and we will continue to be. FOCs, factory outlet centres, are a market development that answers an evident demand. As minister of spatial planning I don't concern myself with that. I do, however, concern myself with where it happens. They should not be isolated stores along the motorway or on the city outskirts, but within the boundaries of the city – no matter whether it's a Bijenkorf department store or one of those FOCs. Thus in Lelystad the factory outlet is to be located on the stretch of land between the coast and the city, on a boulevard that forms a part of the city. There are countless other economic activities that have a great impact on space, for instance the expansion of greenhouse agriculture and the shoebox constructions along the motor-ways.'

'I don't want new construction in the open areas. What I do want is restructuring, the allocation of different functions to existing con-struction. Demolition, yes, but replacement on the same site with something more attractive or smaller. No new estates with Greek columns, but dwellings on an old farm that can no longer survive as a farm. By giving existing buildings new functions we can keep the countryside alive.'

Will the Netherlands look better after the Fifth Report?
'If it's up to me, of course. But not immediately – I'm busy holding back developments that were set in motion 20 years back. Spatial planning is really a tanker, you know. As minister of Spatial Planning I'm not trying to create something new; I don't have a blueprint or ideal that looks vastly different from the Netherlands of today.'

So we can still influence the structure of the Netherlands?
'Oh yes, and it always has been possible. If spa-tial planning were not subject to human influen-ce, then I would be helpless. But then you must not leave it all to economic interests. You must not invest solely in new business sites but also in social processes. There are no uncontrollable developments that you cannot accommodate if you so wish. But it is a hard fight. The great dan-ger, of course, is that capital-heavy actors will brush aside administrators or planners. In that case they are jointly responsible for allowing that to happen. As a civil servant you can better not place too much faith in the clout of capital.'

Glossary

Green Heart Agro-industrial landscape at the center of the circle of cities making up the Randstad.

Paars II or **Purple Coalition** Popular label for the coalition government between the social-democratic Labour Party (PvdA), the liberal People's Party for Freedom and Democracy (VVD), and the liberal-democratic Democrats '66 (D66). The combined house-style colors of the two largest parties, VVD (blue) and PvdA (red), produce the 'purple' designation that has been applied to two successive coalitions headed by the PvdA prime minister Wim Kok since 1994.

Randstad A term coined in the 1930s to describe the ring of cities in the west of the country (Rotterdam/The Hague/Amsterdam/Utrecht) circling what was then a largely undeveloped area, the Green Heart.

Vinex Acronym of the Dutch title of the Supplement to the **Fourth Report on Spatial Planning** (1990). Also used to refer to the urban expansion areas foreshadowed by the Supplement and presently being developed, the so-called Vinex sites.

afvalstort   agrarisch natuurbeheer   beeldentuin   bereikbaarheid   big spotters hill
biologische varkenshouderij   blauwe stad   boerderette   boerennatuur   boom town   borg
ulderbos   businesspark   calamiteitenpolder   carpoolparkeerplaats   compensatiegroen
containeroverslag   corridor   cultuurhistorische identiteit   dagrecreatie
dijkverzwaring   dynamisch kustbeheer   ecologische verbindingszone   eerste maasvlakte
erfafscheiding   euregio   factory outlet   ganzengedoogzone   godshuis   glastuinbouw

De taal van de ruimtelijke ordening Theo Baart
The language of spatial planning

global village   golf course   groene hart   grondgebonden woning   hergebruik
hoge snelheids lijn   ijzeren rijn   jungle dome   knooppunt   lang parkeren   leisure park
ainport   mobiele telefonie   nieuwe natuur   nieuw landgoed   oeververbinding   open gebied
perifere detailhandelsvestiging   rafelrand   railterminal   retro wonen   slotcoördinatie
spookwijk   tweede huis   vernieuwing naoorlogse wijken   vinexlocatie
visuele afscherming snelweg   wadi   waterberging   windmolenpark
winkelgebied   wonen aan het water

Op een voormalige afvalstort is een overdekte skipiste aangelegd.

An indoor ski slope built on a former rubbish tip.

afvalstort

agrarisch natuurbeheer

Boeren krijgen subsidie om de natuur op hun bedrijf te beschermen,
zoals hier in Waterland, ten noorden van Amsterdam.

Farmers receive subsidies for the protection of nature on their land,
as here in Waterland, to the north of Amsterdam.

WATERLAND

Deze camping aan de Noordzeekust werd gesloten vanwege de milieuverontreiniging door de nabijgelegen staalfabriek; nu is het een beeldentuin.

This campsite on the North Sea coast was closed due to the environmental pollution from a neighbouring steelworks; now it is a sculpture garden.

beeldentuin

File op een zomerse zondagavond.

Traffic jam on a summer Sunday evening.

bereikbaarheid

Op de toekomstige land- en tuinbouwtentoonstelling in de Haarlemmermeerpolder, de Floriade, verrijst vlakbij de nieuwe vijfde baan van Schiphol een heuvel vanwaar je de vliegtuigen kunt spotten.

On the site of the coming Floriade horticultural exhibition in the Haarlemmermeer Polder, a hill from which you can spot aeroplanes has emerged close to the new fifth runway at Schiphol Airport.

big spotters hill

Een diervriendelijke, extensieve varkensboerderij.
An animal-friendly, extensive pig farm.

biologische varkenshouderij

HUPPEL 93

Om dit agrarisch gebied in het noorden van Groningen aantrekkelijker te maken voor wonen en recreatie wordt een deel ervan onder water gezet.

blauwe stad

There are plans to flood part of this agricultural area in the north of the province of Groningen in order to make it more attractive for living and recreation.

Nieuwbouw waarvan de vormgeving associaties moet oproepen met een boerderij.
Veel toegepast op vrije kavels.

boerderette

The design of these new buildings is meant to conjure up associations with a farmstead.
It is often used on plots where the homeowners design and built their own house.

Stedelingen zijn welkom op agrarische bedrijven om kennis te maken
met het boerenbedrijf en de landelijkheid.

Agricultural businesses welcome urbanites to introduce them
to life on the farm and the delights of country life.

boerennatuur

WAARDER   99

Een van de snelst groeiende bedrijfsconcentraties van Nederland, vlakbij Schiphol.

boom

One of the fastest-growing concentrations of business activity in the Netherlands, close to Schiphol Airport.

town

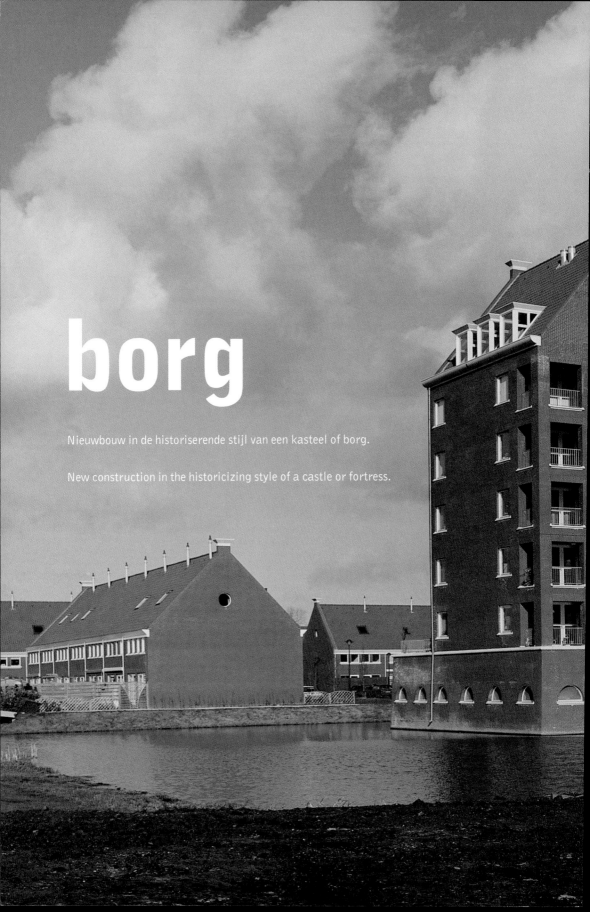

borg

Nieuwbouw in de historiserende stijl van een kasteel of borg.

New construction in the historicizing style of a castle or fortress.

Precies daar waar Schiphol een nieuwe landingsbaan wil aanleggen hebben protesterende milieuorganisaties land gekocht en een 'bos' geplant.

Protesting environmental organizations have bought land exactly where Schiphol Airport intends to construct a new runway and planted a 'wood'.

bulderbos

businesspark

friesland west

Een gebied dat bij extreem hoog water mag onderlopen.

An area permitted to flood when the water level is dangerously high.

calamiteitenpolder

Parkeervoorziening langs de snelweg waar autodelers hun auto
achterlaten om samen in één auto verder te reizen.

Parking along the motorway where car-poolers can leave their cars
in order to make the rest of their journey in a shared car.

carpoolparkeerplaats

A15   111

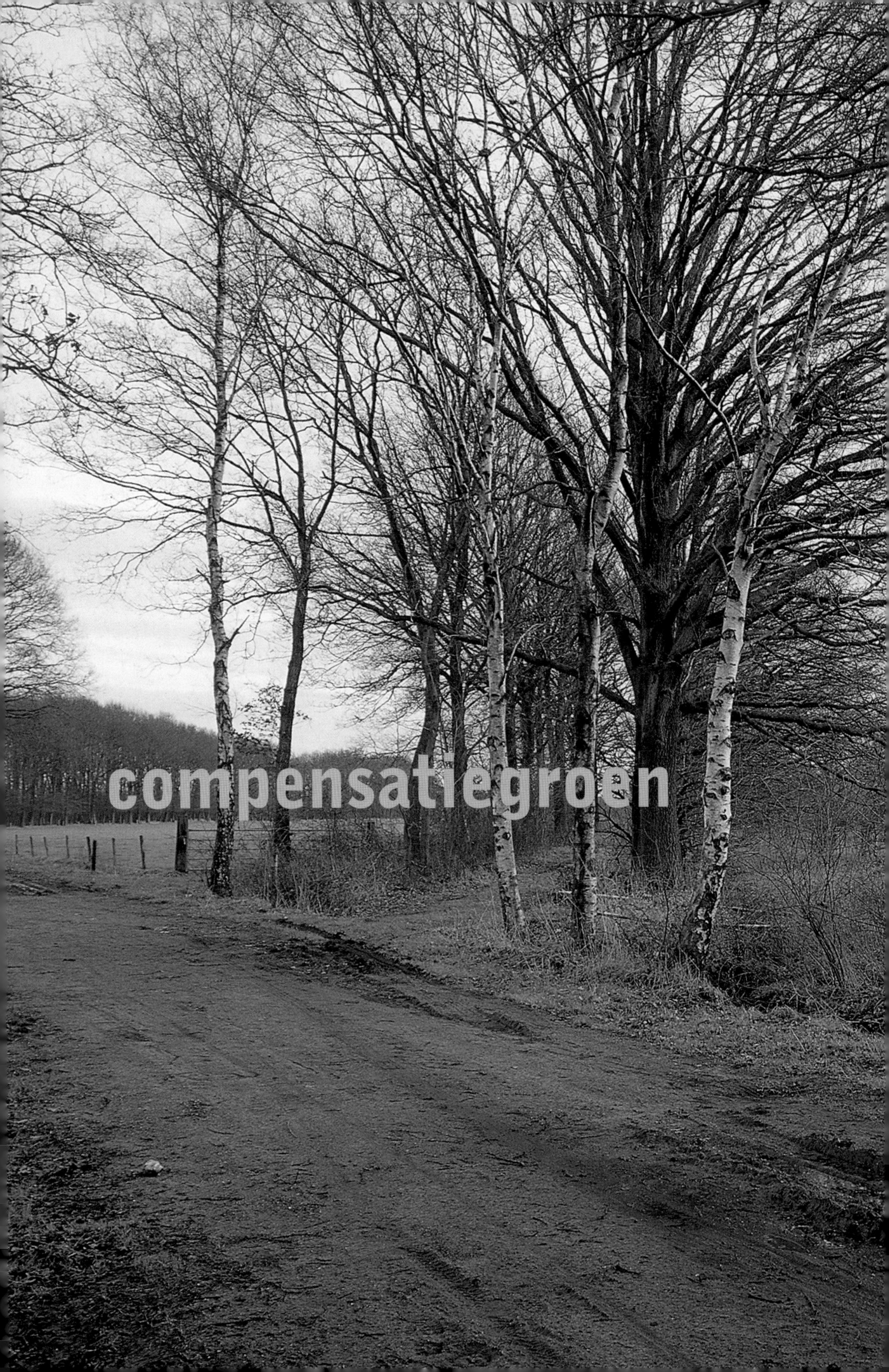
compensatiegroen

Natuur die verloren gaat door de aanleg van infrastructuur wordt
gecompenseerd door de aankoop en aanplant van nieuwe groengebieden.

The acquisition and cultivation of new areas of green compensate nature
that is lost because of the construction of infrastructure.

containeroverslag

Havengebied bij Rotterdam voor overslag van zeecontainers op binnenvaartschepen, treinen of vrachtwagens.

The port area close to Rotterdam for the transhipment of sea containers to barges, trains or lorries.

corridor

Langs de snelwegen ontstaan ketens van kantoorgebouwen en
bedrijfsterreinen voor de distributie en bewerking van goederen.

Ribbons of office buildings and business parks for the distribution
and processing of goods appear along the motorways.

HUNZE

cultuurhistorische identiteit

Twee naburige en toch heel verschillende gebieden in Drenthe, die ieder
door de ontstaansgeschiedenis van het landschap en het gebruik ervan
een eigen herkenbare identiteit hebben ontwikkeld.

Two neighbouring yet completely different areas in the province of Drenthe,
each of which has a distinct and characterful identity influenced by the
development of the landscape and its use.

dagrecreatie

Het voormalige terrein van de land- en tuinbouwtentoonstelling Floriade is ingericht als recreatiegebied.

The former site of the Floriade horticultural exhibition
has been transformed into a recreation area.

GAASPERPLAS, AMSTERDAM   121

dijkverzwaring

De rivierdijken zijn versneld verhoogd of vervangen om de veiligheid te garanderen.

The river dikes have been raised or replaced in order to guarantee safety.

dynamisch kustbeheer

Door een kerf in de duinen kan het zeewater doordringen in het land erachter.
Door het dalen van het land en het stijgen van de zeespiegel is het nodig om
de verdediging van de kust flexibeler te maken.

The seawater can penetrate into the hinterland through a break in the dunes.
The subsiding land and rising sea necessitate a more flexible approach.

ecologische verbindingszone

Aangelegde verbinding tussen twee natuurgebieden.

Man-made connection between two nature areas.

Landwinning voor de kust leverde een groot gebied op voor havenactiviteiten en recreatie.

Land reclamation beyond the coastline created a large area for port activities and recreation.

eerste maasvlakte

In nieuwbouwwijken worden het privé en het openbare door schuttingen gescheiden.

erfafscheiding

In new housing developments, private and public space are demarcated by fences.

In het grensgebied van Nederland en Duitsland worden gebieden
gemeenschappelijk ontwikkeld.

Areas in the border regions between the Netherlands and Germany
are developed jointly.

KERKRADE 133

In een voormalige kazerne komt een grootschalig winkelcentrum
waar fabrikanten hun waren met korting aanbieden.

A former barracks will house a large-scale shopping centre
where manufacturers sell their goods at discounted prices.

factory outlet

Agrarische gebieden waar ganzen met rust worden gelaten worden en de boeren
compensatie krijgen voor de schade die de ganzen met grazen veroorzaken.

Agricultural area where geese are left to graze in peace and the farmers
are compensated for the damage they cause.

ganzengedoogzone

godshuis

WAALWIJK

Glastuinbouw wordt verplaatst om in West-Nederland nieuwe wijken te kunnen bouwen.

glastuinbouw

Greenhouse horticulture is being relocated in order to make way
for new housing developments in the west of the Netherlands.

global village

Voormalige boerderij is getransformeerd tot golfbaan.

Former farm is transformed into a golf course.

golf course

groene hart

Het landelijke gebied tussen de vier grote steden in het westen van Nederland.

The rural area between the four large cities in the west of the Netherlands.

grondgebonden woning

Suburbaan wonen: een woning met een tuin.

Suburban living: a house with a garden.

hergebruik

Snelweg is verlegd en maakt plaats voor bedrijfsterrein.

A motorway is re-routed, making way for a business zone.

hoge snelheids lijn

Grote nieuwe spoorprojecten worden aangelegd voor de Betuwelijn tussen Rotterdam en Duitsland
en de Hoge Snelheids Lijn tussen diverse grote Europese steden.

Large new rail projects under construction for the Betuwe line between Rotterdam and Germany
and the HSL high-speed line between various large European cities.

Historisch tracé van de spoorlijn tussen Antwerpen en het Ruhrgebied dat wellicht nieuw leven wordt ingeblazen.

ijzeren rijn

Historic route of the railway line between Antwerp and the Ruhr industrial zone, Germany, which will possibly be given a new lease of life.

Overdekt subtropisch 'woud' in een vakantiepark.

Indoor subtropical 'forest' in a holiday park.

jungle dome

knooppunt

lang parkeren

Uitgestrekte velden asfalt voor de auto's van luchtreizigers.

Vast fields of asphalt for the cars of air travellers.

leisure park

Een verzameling gebouwen aan de rand van de stad met daarin
verschillende attracties, waaronder veel elektronisch amusement.

A collection of buildings on the edge of the city with a range of
attractions, including a great deal of electronic amusement.

mainport

mobiel

A2
Zendmasten langs snelwegen voor de mobiele telefonie.

elefonie

Masts alongside motorways for mobile telecommunications.

nieuwe natuur

MILLINGERWAARD

Voormalig agrarisch gebied wordt landgoed met villa's.

Former agricultural land is turned into a country estate with villas.

nieuw landgoed

Nieuwe bruggen en tunnels verbinden voormalige havengebieden met het stadscentrum.

New bridges and tunnels connect former harbour areas with the city centre.

oeververbinding

open gebied

Zoetwaterreservoir en recreatiegebied. Freshwater reservoir and recreation area.

perifer

Weidewinkels en meubelboulevards langs snelwegen en uitvalswegen.

Hypermarkets and furniture stores alongside motorways and arterial roads.

VENLO 177

rafelrand

De rommelige overgang tussen bebouwing en het landelijk gebied.

The haphazard transition from suburban to rural.

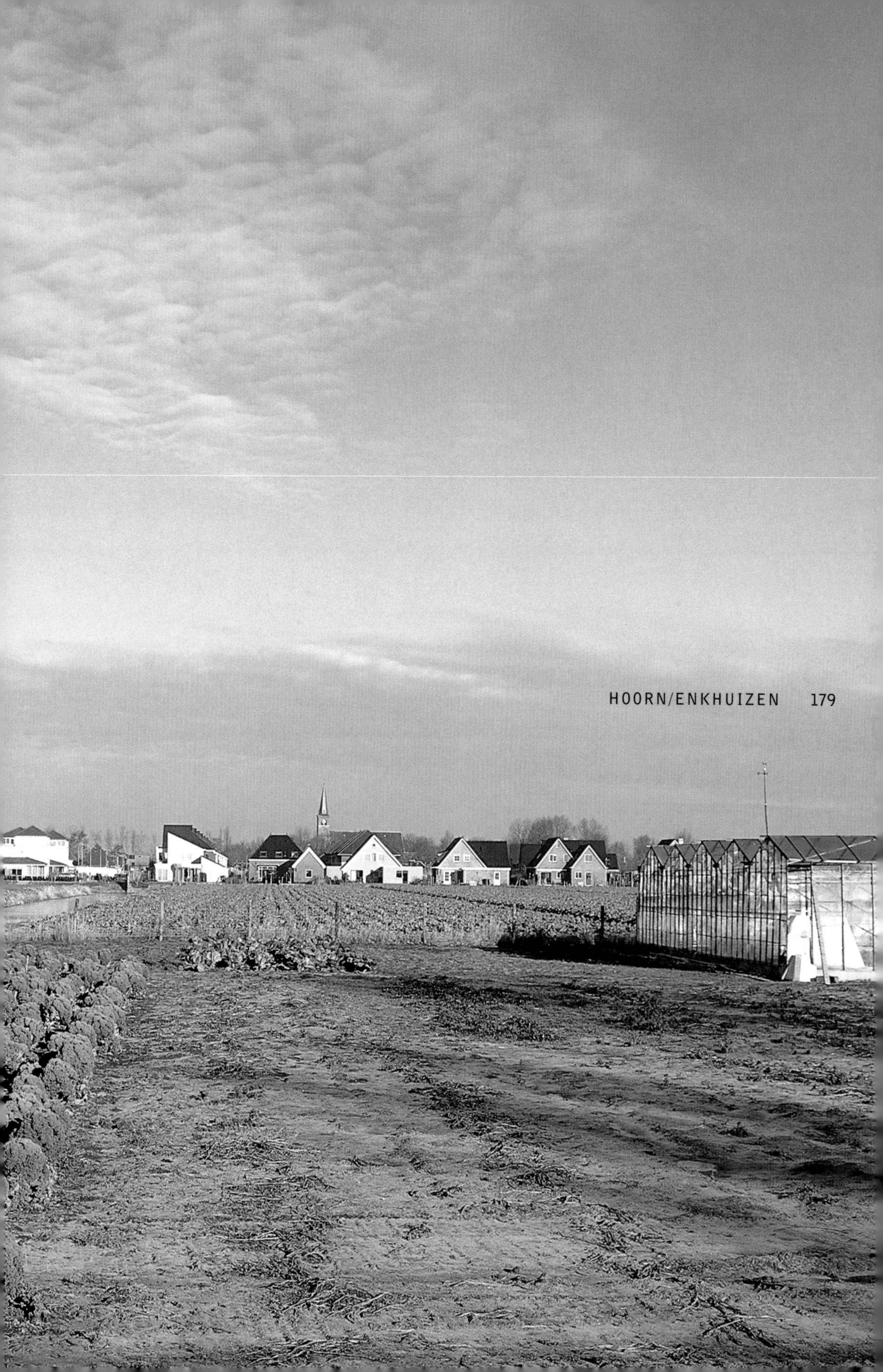

Overslag van treincontainers naar vrachtwagens.

Transfer of train containers to lorries.

railterminal

VENLO   181

Nieuwbouw in de stijl van de jaren dertig van de twintigste eeuw.

New housing in the style of the 1930s.

retro wonen

slotcoördinatie

Drukte in het luchtruim wordt beheerst door te reguleren hoeveel vliegtuigen
wanneer mogen landen en opstijgen.

Congestion in the air is controlled by regulating how many aircraft
are permitted to take off and land, and when.

spookwijk

Woonwijk wordt gesloopt omdat deze niet meer aan te passen is
aan de veranderende woonwensen.

Housing estate being demolished because it could no longer be adapted
to satisfy the changing housing preferences.

Nederlanders compenseren gebrek aan ruimte en rust door een
betaalbaar tweede huis in of buiten Nederland te kopen.

tweede huis

Residents of the Netherlands compensate for the lack of space and quiet by buying an affordable second home within or outside the Netherlands.

Hoogbouw uit de jaren zestig wordt gesloopt om plaats te maken voor huizen met een tuin.

High-rise from the 1960s is demolished to make way for houses with a garden.

AMSTERDAM-ZUIDOOST   191

Grote nieuwbouwwijken nabij de bestaande steden zoals is verordonneerd in de Vierde Nota Ruimtelijke Ordening.

vinexlocatie

Large new housing estates close to existing urban centres, as prescribed in the Fourth Report on Spatial Planning in the Netherlands.

Schermen langs de snelwegen die de geluidsoverlast beperken en het zicht op de snelweg ontnemen.

Bafflers along the motorway that reduce noise pollution and hide the motorway from view.

visuele afsch

A12   195

ming snelweg

wadi

Gesloten systeem binnen een wijk voor de waterhuishouding.

A self-contained, neighbourhood water-management system.

waterberging

Rivieren worden verbreed om te voorkomen dat ze bij hoog water buiten hun oevers treden.

Rivers are broadened to prevent them breaking their banks when water levels are high.

GRENSMAAS LIMBURG   199

Winning van elektriciteit door grote windmolens.

windmolenpark

Electricity production by large windmills.

ALMERE   201

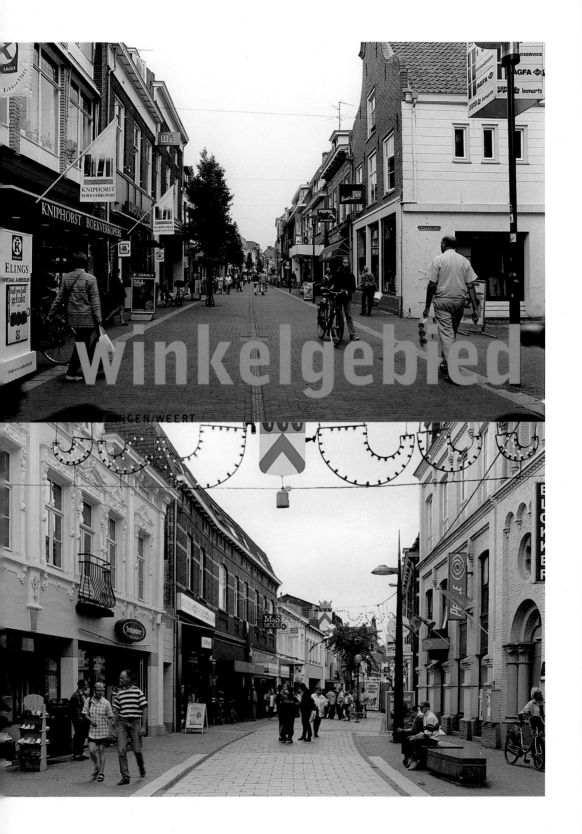

Buiten Amsterdam in het IJ verrijst op een kunstmatige eiland
een grote woonwijk waarbij het wonen aan het water centraal staat.

A large residential development where the focus is on living on the water
is being constructed on an artificial island in the IJ river near Amsterdam.

wonel

an het water

The topography of daily life

Tjerk Ruimschotel

Second Report on Spatial Planning in the Netherlands (1966)

Structural view of the Netherlands in a wider context

The Netherlands as a found landscape

The photographs by Theo Baart, the reportages and interviews by Tracy Metz and the map models by Must do not simply offer an impression of the changes in our country, but most especially capture the way in which we experience this country. That is by no means the same for everyone everywhere at every moment; each of the permanent or temporary inhabitants of the Netherlands carries his or her own personal impression of the country. The majority of residents and users perceive it as if it were an accidentally found landscape, without realizing that the current manifestation of practically every square metre we see today was planned in one way or another. Of course this is a process that has taken centuries, during which time both the struggle with the water and the struggle to establish an autonomous state formed the land on which we live and moulded the country where we live. It was primarily in the postwar period that the Netherlands was transformed into the land that we know today. The 'outlook' of the Dutch population has also altered radically during recent decades, most especially in its increasing breadth. Prosperity has facilitated unprecedented and mass mobility, with all the consequences for the radius of activity of large parts of society. The way in which we utilize the ever-changing Netherlands could play a more influential role in the planning of the future of the country's space than the actual physical land-use. More important than quantitative use of space (if necessary, things can be stacked up) is a qualitative planning in which some places are filled in and others left empty, where it is busy at certain times and congested at others.

The **Fifth Report on Spatial Planning** concerns the government's planned intervention in spatial and physical planning processes over the next thirty years. It is enlightening to look back at what has happened in the Netherlands during the last thirty years, and to ask ourselves whether this is due to, or indeed in spite of this planning policy. In the course of the last century there were countless visionary spatial plans that were focused on the millennium. But when the year 2000 came around it turned out to be a bit of a damp squib as a watershed. The Netherlands did not see any big millennium clean-up – not even a small-scale evaluation of the last century. The **Fifth Report** is only a further step in the continuing process that has always defined the physical planning of the Netherlands, most especially in the twentieth century. In this country of cities, this is a process still concerned with managing the relationship between town and countryside – in short the urbanization process. Reality often turns out to be different to what the paper-trail of plan formulation and the political decision-making process would have us believe. The Schiphol Airport railway link, for example, has not resulted in the faster connection times expected; the port of Delfzijl has not become the thriving industrial zone that the government intended; businesses have not followed the residential developments to the suburbs, as was predicted in the mid-1970s.

In and of itself there is nothing wrong with this. As many a designer has concluded when confronted with the built result of a plan with which they have not been involved for some time: 'Well, I guess that's also a possibility.'

On the one hand, this may be disheartening; on the other, the constant questioning of conclusions already made is a healthy antidote to the gradual narrowing of vision and megalomania that typifies the planning process. Planning in the 1970s was especially culpable of embarassing mistakes, such as the large-scale urban renewal projects, the Hoog Catherijne shopping centre in Utrecht, and the Utrechtse Baan city highway in The Hague. We can count ourselves lucky that many of the planned large-scale reconstruction projects here in the Netherlands have not been realized. The machinery is in fact kept ticking over by this continuous tinkering, but the machine operators have an ever-greater need for an instruction manual.

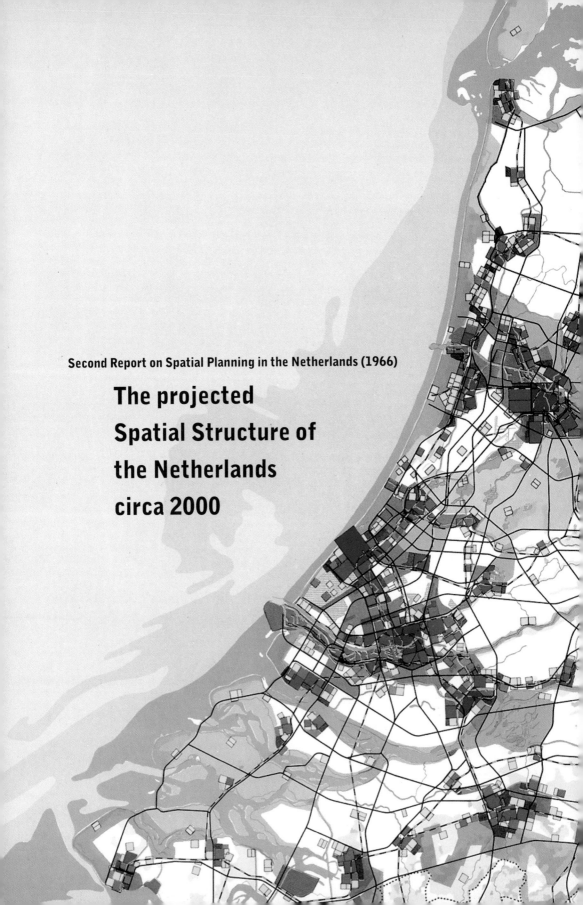

Second Report on Spatial Planning in the Netherlands (1966)

The projected
Spatial Structure of
the Netherlands
circa 2000

Navigating the globe, travelling in time

We make more and more use of maps, not only to reach the destination for our annual vacation, but also in our daily lives, for example if we want to avoid a traffic jam or are visiting friends and family who have moved to newly built housing estates. Some fast-growing cities such as Almere have published new city maps every year for the last twenty years. The exclusive logic of the traffic systems makes it is less and less advisable to trust your instinctive sense of direction. With Internet travel sites and other advanced tools such as talking on-board navigation computers in cars, we make our way to destinations that are no longer found where you might have expected them to be in days gone by: the large shops are on the ringroad, there are cafes in the party centre at the business park as well as on the church square, and the prostitutes don't just stand behind glass in the Red Light district, the Wallen, but also at designated out-of-town prostitution zones. There is also an increase in the number of events. These do not only have their own special signposting, as with the European football championships, but also occasionally make whole urban districts (in)accessible: Queen's Day in Amsterdam, the Rotterdam Marathon, the Bloemencorso flower parade in the Bollenstreek bulb-growing area, the book market on the banks of the IJssel river in Deventer, or the national con-vention held by Libelle women's magazine in Almere. The unsuspecting traveller encounters more and more traffic congestion and delays in places where they are usually not to be found. The information in newspapers and magazines is increasingly accompanied by brightly coloured little maps, charting the weather for today and tomorrow, the yearly flurry of Royal Decorations, the location of the new nature areas, the level of local taxes, the alternative locations for Schiphol Airport, and other calamities.

Mental map Alongside or sometimes instead of these paper (and digital) maps we always carry our own personal impression of the world around with us: a kind of virtual map in our mind, a mental map. This internal record of the world around us bears only a fleeting resemblance to the geographical reality we are familiar with from the trusted topographical maps, or to the boundaries of administrative territories such as municipality, province and kingdom. We now need a sign such as 'Welcome to our province' or 'Welcome to our borough', because from the motorway or from the tram you would not notice the broder crossing. If we were to diagrammatically capture our personal 'window' on the world it would create an image of our individual environment and how we relate (geographically) to other people and territories. This mental map is a polymorphous hamlet, made up of isolated and mutually overlapping places and interconnections, some sharply defined, others blurred or barely detectable. This perceived image of our environment is coloured by memories and adapted according to our day-to-day experiences. By travelling, even if it is just in reading a book at home, the traveller creates a landscape as a succession of places and the emotions evoked by these places.

Such as it once was, nowadays in any case there is no absolute or discernible spatio-functional distinction between town and country. Instead of a static way of life we have a dynamic living pattern. Because we are continuously on the move it is possible to discover new places all the time, requalify one's own position and adopt new identities. The individual mental map of the Netherlander is but one of the tools for this navigation through space and time. It is increasingly common to receive road directions or a description of public transport connections along with a letter of invitation. Soon you will be able to call it up on the display of your mobile telephone, and nowadays even children have a personal organizer and a city map in their pocket. Thematic guidebooks and manuals are being published on every imaginable activity. Mobility has become the cultural expression of our time.

The home as a base of operations For a long time planners and politicians thought that the Netherlander faced the world via concentric circles increasing in size and anonymity as they emanated from the home base: the street, the neighbourhood, the district, the town, along with its hierarchy ranging from the everyday (baker, butcher, grocer) to the more incidental facilities and conveniences (theatre, wholesalers). After the war, this traditional neighbourhood- and district-delimited environment gradually made way for a much more complex overlapping of multifarious horizons. These were in part fed by experiences, picked up while travelling (on vacation) through the Netherlands and beyond, and partly determined by the ever expanding circuit of regions and events covered by the press. In addition, the ethno-cultural backgrounds of an increasing number of Dutch citizens is no longer limited to culture indigenous to regions within the geographical borders of the Netherlands. Citizens are less and less restricted in their choice of place to live and work, and the whole world is more and more open to them for their recreation.

There can be no discussion about how 'full' the Netherlands is without mentioning the growing number of opportunities to claim our own space and time, i.e. be able to make use of other territories at self-determined moments, with one's own home as an operational base. For someone who can regularly go out, the home base is less oppressively full than for someone who is condemned to the limited space of the home or living environment. These days we simultaneously experience a global and a very local sense of space and time. And in fact because there are fewer restrictive external factors that determine our choice of living or workplace, these places will have to be differentiated by specific characteristics. This localization goes hand in hand with a growing awareness that each place is but one of the many on this planet. That was made clear on the eve of the new millennium, as it was celebrated by each time zone in turn. Never before was there such a mass awaress that we inhabit a single globe with so many easily accessible places. The world briefly seemed like a village, but everyone stayed at home.

The struggle for space In this age of peace, prosperity and new technology, we must not forget the struggle that was the real historic background of our built culture. The struggle against the water, against the treachery of nature, against hunger and misery, against social discrimination and exclusion, against the unchallenged right of the economically strong. If war is a form of politics but with other means, then spatial planning is a form of war using memoranda and reports as weapons. In the final analysis, spatial planning is also about the appropriation of land and space, i.e. the use of the land. In other parts of the world this struggle is played out with force of arms; in the Netherlands there are laws and covenants to keep this to a less bloody arena. In what the journalist H.J.A. Hofland once called the 'planological civil war', the physical planning maps have taken over the function of the military ordnance survey maps. In the run-up to the **Fifth Report on Spatial Planning**, the cabinet has sparked a little frenzy of land-grabbing by suggesting an ominous shortage of living space. The inventory of all the bids for land over the next 30 years indicated that the demand for new land would cover an area the size of the province of South-Holland. Spoilt by the availability or proximity of goods and services, we barely have the time to wait for anything, especially in the Randstad. In the quest to find the shortest, and above all the fastest routes, the infrastructure is stacked up, so that the various streams of traffic can proceed unhindered. Alongside bridges, tunnels and aqueducts for the cars, people, bikes and ships, there are new flyovers or underpasses being constructed – in the form of badger tunnels and ecoducts – where the road infrastructure and the Ecological Mainframe intersect. Instead of being allowed to experience the beauty of the Green Heart, speeding train passengers are funnelled through a tunnel, so that the cows can continue to enjoy the pastoral landscape in peace. Functions that cannot work well when placed alongside each other are increasingly being constructed on top of each other, with the newest usage (almost always regarded as the disruptive element) is usually stowed away below ground level. The Netherlands, the Lowlands, is becoming a land of layers: the Layerlands.

In the Dutch pavilion at the Expo 2000 world's fair in Hanover, Germany, all kinds of different ways of using space are literally stacked one on top of the other in a towering construction more than 40 metres high. This is a striking metaphor for the spatio-functional problem in our land. The stacking of landscapes is an architectonic illustration of the quite absurd situation that would arise if all the country's spatial demands (in the areas of energy supply, water management, flower-bulb cultivation, food supply, space for dwellings and work, holiday resorts, waste disposal, nature area, and so on) were to be satisfied within the borders of the Netherlands simultaneously. This intensive use of land does have a certain attraction in an urban environment, though it calls to mind strong associations with the megalomaniac constructions that were meant to do away with the spatial planning problems in the 1960s and '70s.

**The New Map of
the Netherlands
1997**

Town and country – the changing Netherlands from 1965 and 2000

The Netherlands can be seen either as a densely populated country or as a sparsely populated city in the West-European delta. This is not merely a play on words: many so-called problems vanish when considered on a larger scale. Apparently this is primarily a question of definition. Many people place the blame for a number of societal problems in questions of ethnicity (immigrants, asylum seekers) and technical areas (manure surplus, housing shortage, road congestion), on the limited size of the Netherlands, the extent of the spatial claims and the feeling of congestion that this creates. In order to understand what has actually changed (and improved) we will take the mid-1960s as our reference point, when the Central Bureau for Statistics (CBS) predicted that the population of the Netherlands would increase from the then 12.5 million to 20 million by the year 2000. This frightening prognosis led to serious suggestions from the world of science to radically spread the population across the country. In addition to a Randstad with 6 million residents (about the same number as now), the countryside would have to accommodate 14 million people, 11 million of whom in a limited number of regional concentrations. Five cities – Groningen, Leeuwarden, Venlo, Den Bosch and Roosendaal-Bergen op Zoom – would expand to populations of 600,000 and there would be three city mergers with 700,000 residents, christened with new names such as Rhine and Waal City (the Arnhem-Nijmegen coupling), IJssel City (the triangle Apeldoorn, Deventer and Zutphen) and Twente City (Hengelo, Enschede and Almelo). The presumed dynamism of this 'dispersion policy' is put into perspective if we consider that Eindhoven, which has yet to reach 200,000 residents, currently has the largest population concentration outside the Randstad. And then to think that Meppel, with 30,000 residents, and Tilburg, with 190,000, are the smallest and biggest of the fourteen places that were supposed to develop into urban centres with more than 450,000 residents, the current population of The Hague.

Oppressive congestion The government went a long way toward this solution in the Second Report on Spatial Planning of 1966, except that the 20 million people were divided between a somewhat larger number of cores, which meant that it was more in line with the traditional size of Dutch towns and cities. An excessive dispersion of the population was held back by the planning hallmark of the Second Report, specifically 'bundled deconcentration'. The intention was that different cores would together form a metropolitan district. The entire physical layout of existing cities and new extensions was schematically constructed out of four living environments, visually represented by little blocks of various colour and size. These abstract units helped to find a realistic spatial map of the way in which the population could be housed. This 'block map' showed that there was sufficient space for 20 million people to live, work and recreate in an attractive environment, an environment also occasionally expressly kept open and undeveloped. To provide all those Dutch people in the twenty-first century with the opportunity to call on

one another, a network of roadways was projected across the whole country, an infrastructure that explicitly related to what was christened 'The Netherlands-City'.

This highway network loosely draped across the land has not been realized according to plan. A number of connections were scrapped, others were grafted as much as possible onto the existing road network that went from city to city. Because of this most cities got a ringroad, which creates traffic jams because traffic that is going to the city is mixed with traffic that wants to pass it by. In addition, the national motorway and railway network is more than ever becoming entangled with building development, with residential neighbourhoods being constructed right up to or even above the infrastructure these days. The outcome – often unintentional – is that the journey no longer goes through the country and past the cities, but is interrupted again and again by little towns. This makes it seem as if the Netherlands is fuller than it actually is.

New spatial uses The Second Report painted an almost moving image of a Beautiful Netherlands in 2000, where fathers would commute to new offices and factories by bike, mothers performed their housework neatly, and children played happily in specially-equipped little playgrounds. In the weekend and on holiday, people drove their little cars to find peace and open space in the park-like countryside or in recreation areas on the edge of town.

Instead of this balanced and well-cared-for arrangement, our country at the turn of the millennium is a picture of continuous reconstruction, with half-complete projects and newly devised solutions for already long irrelevant problems: the whole country is constantly being 'broken up'. The number of cars is lower than predicted because the population has not increased that fast. There are all manner of new uses that the legends of national planning maps do not yet include: recreational dwelling, water storage, geese tolerance zones, compensatory green. That came to light in 1997, when the 'New Map of the Netherlands' inventorized all the plans to be realized through 2010. Almost every plan was justified by its presumed 'synergetic' effect, through which conflicting interests could be served simultaneously. New terms such as 'combined recreational use', 'farmland nature area' and 'nature area creation through urbanization' show that physical and spatial projects are moving further and further beyond the traditional categories. It becomes really complex when all kinds of new spaces are also used in different and sometimes unexpected ways. Today, it is increasingly difficult for planners and government bodies to determine whether there is too much or too little of anything, be it dwellings, nature or business zones.

There is undoubtedly an evolution going on in spatial in-fill that leads one to suspect there is a completely new 'human ecology'. The nature, characteristics and the distribution patterns of this new use of space are no longer specific to one particular place. The use of space is more and more something that is fluid, as it were. People live in warehouse and farmhouses, stopping places for business meetings and erotic encounters appear along the motorway. A stone pier on the IJ river in Amsterdam serves as a passenger terminal, becomes a transhipment store for coal, a port of call for navy ships, a berth for student boats, and is then reincarnated as a neighbourhood entertainment complex. That is why the mental maps of the residents of the Netherlands are so richly multifarious and continually subject to change.

Not only have there been a great deal of physical changes within the borders of the Netherlands, mobility has also radically altered the way in which we use the spatial structure. The outcome is a paradox: on the one hand the Netherlands has become more accessible, and thus perceived as smaller, on the other, the range of places and environments from which we can choose has increased enormously, which means that we simultaneously experience the Netherlands as bigger and more richly varied. Nonetheless, many people feel that the continuing extension of the contemporary use of space is at the expense of the unspoilt 'archetypical' Dutch landscape. The government presumes that it can limit the spatial problems to what people refer to as 'already spoilt' areas with restrictive policy. In recent decades there has been an about-turn in the evaluation of urban expansion and agricultural modernization: practically every planning application involving change or modernization is met with objections. The civic pride in the massive housing production, large-scale enterprise and endless road construction of the post-war years has been superseded by fear and loathing.

The paradox of the Second Report and the disappearance of the inhabitant

Until the mid-1960s there was some degree of consensus about the objective and limits of spatial planning as a government activity. The solutions for the problems in the first decennia after the Second World War were barely a topic of discussion in society: reconstruction of the ravaged Netherlands and a search for compensation for the loss of the Netherlands Indies. After the cabinet fell in 1965, in the 'Night of Schmelzer', the next cabinet, though of a completely different political persuasion, was able to adopt the same **Second Report** almost unchanged. Things are different now. Planning policy is politicized and is a high priority on the social agenda, but the legitimacy of the government to execute it is more and more often questioned. The generally felt urgency of the problem calls for forceful government direction. But the greatest need is for an administrator with a mind for logistics and **crowd control**; not an artistic director. Spatial planning is less and less a question of the composition of the space, and more and more about the regulation of the use of the space by large groups.

The problem, in short, lies in the fact that we are still insufficiently open to the mass character accepteren of the democratization of the creature comforts that fifty years ago were the preserve of only a small class: creature comforts in the home, a getaway in the great outdoors for the summer, good education and training, adequate work conditions and sufficient opportunities to partake in sport, recreation and vacation. Advocates of limiting the use of space, reducing energy consumption, and less mobility find an attractive and spacious

The Netherlands 2030 – Consultative Report, Explorations of Spatial Perspectives

National overview of four landscape perspectives: palette, park, flows and urbanization

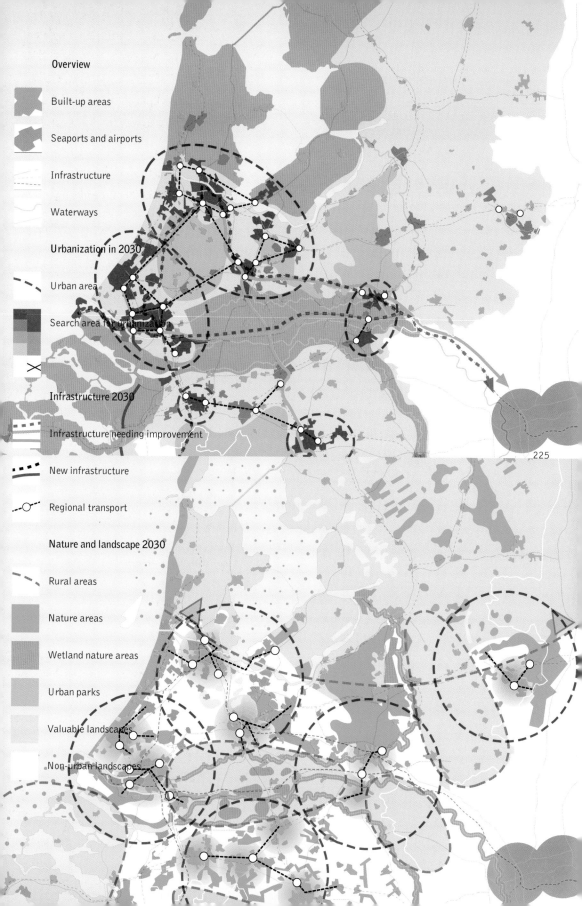

Overview

Built-up areas

Seaports and airports

Infrastructure

Waterways

Urbanization in 2030

Urban area

Search area for urbanization

Infrastructure 2030

Infrastructure needing improvement

New infrastructure

Regional transport

Nature and landscape 2030

Rural areas

Nature areas

Wetland nature areas

Urban parks

Valuable landscapes

Non-urban landscapes

living environment and a certain social, cultural and recreational mobility so important in their own private domain that they (just like the majority of their compatriots) expend a great deal of time, money and energy on it.

The experiential world of the citizen As post-war reconstruction was nearing completion in the mid-1960s, the **Second Report** formulated the first comprehensive image of the territory of the Netherlands. And as the future spatial order gained the status of a socio-political problem, the general public was given the opportunity to offer its input and views in a political and social sense. This led to a discussion – which is now becoming more heated – about whether the proposed government policy would result in the most auspicious spatial arrangement of the Netherlands.

Because the government has recently harmed or threatened to harm the living environment of citizens due to lack of care (Amelisweerd, Shell-Moerdijk, Kalkar), government policy, in part thanks to persistent protest, finds itself in a permanent process of manipulation, compromise and policy creation. Spatial planning has become an interactive news column.

Spatial planning should be concerned with establishing a balanced relationship between the people and their habitat or biotope. It is urprising then that government policy as a social instrument is becoming ever further removed from solutions for everyday problems. In the policy documents residents have literally disappeared from the picture. While around the time of the **Second Report** there was continual mention of the number of residents who had to

be housed, by the time of the **Fifth Report** the only unit of measurement being mentioned is the number of dwellings and the area occupied by business zones or nature areas. Instead of the rather naïve aspirations extant during the 1960s and '70s to create complete and pleasing living environments, today's quest is to find suitable locations for residential construction. There is no longer any relation between the way in which individual residents and businesspeople on the one hand, and the different layers of government and landowners on the other, make their decisions. The sometimes inscrutable decision-making processes and compromises that take place in every municipality and province are not important to average citizens; for them it is the outcome that is essential. For a municipal councillor, the link between the levying of tolls on the one road and the construction of a new road elsewhere are part and parcel of a coherent package of measures to solve mobility problems around the city. The car driver who only uses the toll road does not understand the advantage of the other road that is being financed with his or her tolls.

The limitations of the spatial planning policy Where the political administrator sees a scrupulously balanced and all-encompassing decision-making process (here a little more, there a little less, like this here, but like that there), the citizen runs up against the wall of planning legislation. Construction is only permitted within the building line; the growth of village and city is only allowed within the specified contour. You may establish your home without restriction where that is permitted, living in the wild is only allowed in the designated areas. Everyone has to seek his or her own highly personal path between law and reality.

As soon as a normal citizen becomes a politician or planner, he or she knows how to justify the necessity of this restrictive planning policy with the argument that it is in the public interest. Residents, on the other hand, want an affordable house and fast, and then preferably one that resembles those in magazines such as Home & Residence or Gracious Living. Spatial planning capitalizes on this with arguments in favour of home ownership, the development of the catalogue dwelling, the thematic arrangement of public space and differentiation of the living environment. Current affairs magazines and consumer guides have seized on this trend and publish comparative consumer research about the most peaceful, affordable, safe and economically attractive place to live.

It is remarkable that people now hardly ever choose their place of residence on the basis of traditional criteria such as social, cultural, medical and educational facilities. It is as if the residents treat the government plans as a stack of catalogues listing the possibilities for living, working, leisure, mobility and earning money. We can perceive the Netherlands itself as a kind of wholesale supermarket where you can shop around for one product after the other. Many collective arrangements have actually or psychologically become invisible: the most basic reason to form a community was that a collective defence was more effective than an individual one. The need for the protection of town walls and defensive lines has gradually become superfluous. Communal utilities such as telephone, gas, water, electricity, postal delivery, cable TV, district heating and public transport have already been or are soon to be privatized, i.e. 'put on the market'. This renders the legitimacy of a government that exclusively regulates collectivity within its own territory increasingly questionable. There seems to be something of a rift between the politically formulated spatial problem and the social playing field where a solution has to be sought. As far as the inhabitants are concerned, the space in which to answer warranted demands and aspirations does not necessarily have to be found within the chance boundaries of the traditional layers of public administration; new problems also often require cross-border solutions.

Zapping in the United Kingdom of the Republics of the Netherlands

The traditional administrative layout and the landscape profile originally based on the needs of agriculture are no longer adequate. The whole of the Netherlands has become one urban oriented landscape incorporating all kinds of fragments, which are continually adapted to suit new circumstances. For the inhabitants of this continually changing Netherlands, their address is also the outward expression of a temporary operational base. Alongside the actual home and work address, there are ever more places where someone is contactable: e-mail, mobile telephone, business hotels, a little place in the country. Nowadays we have more than just one residential or temporary address. It is this delocalization of the permanent address that causes the need for a concrete image. An address on the Internet isn't called a site for nothing, and many of them are metaphorically constructed as a town with squares and streets. There also seems to be a need to 'chart' the virtual traffic and the abstract structure of the Internet; a site such as www.geography.com offers wonderful illustrations of this.

The address landscapes In contrast with this concretization of the virtual address is the increasing sentimentality about the real address. It is not just cities or regions that try to find an appealing and easily memorable identity, even whole urban districts, neighbourhoods and streets, are often christened with thematically or pseudo-historically laden names: The North, The Foreland, The 13th Province, The Empty Land, Leiden-on-the-Rhine. Both these tendencies reflect the emergence of new, sometimes temporary territories. These new landscapes have their own, but non-exclusive logic. That is how we descry all the contours of the suburban city-scape of the urbanized West (the Delta Metro-polis) within which the networking citizen can live and work. Big sections of the country, such as the coast, the islands, the IJssel Valley and the Achterhoek, are being amalgamated into a landscape for consumption and experience, characterized by the horses and other 'traditional' hobby livestock behind quaint white fences, maintained by and for none other than the urbanites. In addition we can already see the beginnings of the cultural-historic landscape reserves appearing in the hyper-urban peripheries of the Randstad (the Glory of the Historical Inner Cities) on the basis of the **Belvedere Report**, as well as in the reconstruction of defensive landscapes such as the Defence Line of Amsterdam and the New Holland Water Defence Line. Nature conservation organizations have recently been calling for the designation of areas where natural features are the **guiding** principle for the permitted form of dwelling, industry and agriculture. In spatial terms the Netherlands of the twenty-first century is no longer a unified and hierarchically organized kingdom, as it was in the nineteenth century when the territory was first mapped out comprehensively. Since the mid-twentieth century, our country has been more like a continually changing collection of 'republics' or self-organizing groups of citizens. The inhabitant has many complementary and overlapping identities and can simultaneously be a member of (sometimes partly contradictory) interest groups, for example the ANWB automobile club, the Cyclists Association, the Society for the Preservation of Nature in the Netherlands, and the Wadden Conservation Group. He or she can simultaneously be a motorist, train commuter, family visitor or seeker of peace and quiet, or easily switch from one to the other.

Towards a land full of Netherlands The modern tourism industry and cartography are more and more geared to a land full of Netherlands. They produce a continuously changing stream of guides and guidebooks: Nature Reserve maps, Birdwatching maps, a Map of The Hague for the Businessman, inline skating guides, architecture guidebooks. The newspapers have thematic supplements and there is a burgeoning stream of strikingly designed printed material with tips for children's shops, antiquarian booksellers, in short fun-shopping. Instead of the country being organized in a regimented, integrated manner, a collection of National Netherlands for Interest Groups is taking shape. Each Netherland is created again and again, anew, by the people themselves and their day-to-day use of it, in relation to the memory of how it used to be and in hopeful anticipation of what is to come. The pursuit of an integrated and regionally valid plan, as physical zoning plans are by definition, or, as the **Second Report** intended, obliges the different legislative bodies to strive to mould a unified spatial arrangement. But perhaps the planners and politicians should seek out ambiguous land-use allocations in which the eventual constructed result is more a welcome surprise than a pre-programmed execution of the planning map.

Instead of concerning itself with restriction, governmental planning should rather be concerned with stimulation. The government must create opportunities so that the citizen can try to capitalize according to their own tastes and views. The design for the spatial planning of the Netherlands could then consist of a stacking-up of a number of relatively autonomous aspects. In a manner of speaking, the Plan for the New Netherlands consists exclusively in a virtual, digital form, so that every resident of, or visitor to the Netherlands can construct their own country by switching the specific layers of the legend of interest to him or her on or off. Then there are as many Netherlands as there are Netherlanders.

Mapping a changing Netherlands Must

The work of engineering artistry that is the Netherlands seems virtually complete. The great Zuiderzee and Delta projects have been completed; every scrap of land has been reclaimed and opened up for use by efficient agriculture, good employment locations, functional housing environments and ecological key areas. Nothing more can stand in the way of an effective use of the Dutch landscape in its entirety, thanks to a dense web of motorways, roads and railway lines that provide coverage and access throughout the whole of the Netherlands.

While everyone was hard at work making their own little contribution to the completion of this utilitarian landscape, the use of space in the Netherlands has been slowly but radically changing. Order, security and safety have become the unquestioned starting-points for everyone's living environment, and aspects such as freedom, adventure and enjoyment have thus increasingly become the underlying motivation for our behaviour. The corner grocer has often been replaced by a large enclosed shopping mall, complete with 'Coca-Cola oasis', where buying impulses are not guided by the utility or need for an article, but by the seduction of excess. The sober, controlled Netherlands is evolving into a challenging new Netherlands where consumption, personal enjoyment and leisure will be the determining factors in the way it is planned.

The individual's perception of this new Netherlands gives it many different faces. In fact the country cannot be captured in a single image; each individual composes his or her own experiential world, constructed out of the various places that fall within the ambit of the individual living environment. The car, the airplane, but most especially the telephone and the Internet have made it possible to add new locations to our experiential world, no longer limiting it to the Netherlands, Europe or even the world.

In this series of maps, the changing view of the Netherlands is set out as seen from three different angles: new space, new usage forms and new users. This deliberately does not strive to provide a complete or representative rendering of the actual spatial and physical changes in the Netherlands. We opted for a narrative and suggestive presentation of spatial patterns, usage forms and personal world views that are illustrative of this evolving perception.

The first series of maps deals with several spatial changes in the Netherlands between 1966, when the **Second Report on Spatial Planning** was published, and 2000, on the eve of the publication of the **Fifth Report on Spatial Planning.** The second series covers the results of a thematic sample of contemporary usage forms. The third series represents a trio of individual experiential worlds that concern the use of time and space, formed not on the basis of an objective topographic image but along the lines of entirely personal mental constructions.

New space

The increase in **built-up surface** area between 1966 and 2000: new residential neighbourhoods, business parks and shopping centres.

The development of the **infrastructure** between 1966 and 2000: a phenomenal expansion of the motorway network compared with moderate development of the railways.

The **reduction of the openness** between 1966 and 2000: fragmentation and densification due to the disappearance of agricultural land and open water.

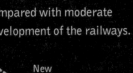 Expansion of built-up area

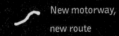 New rail route

 Reduction of open water

 New motorway, new route

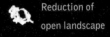 Reduction of open landscape

New motorway, existing route

 Reduction of sidewing landscape

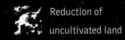 Reduction of uncultivated land

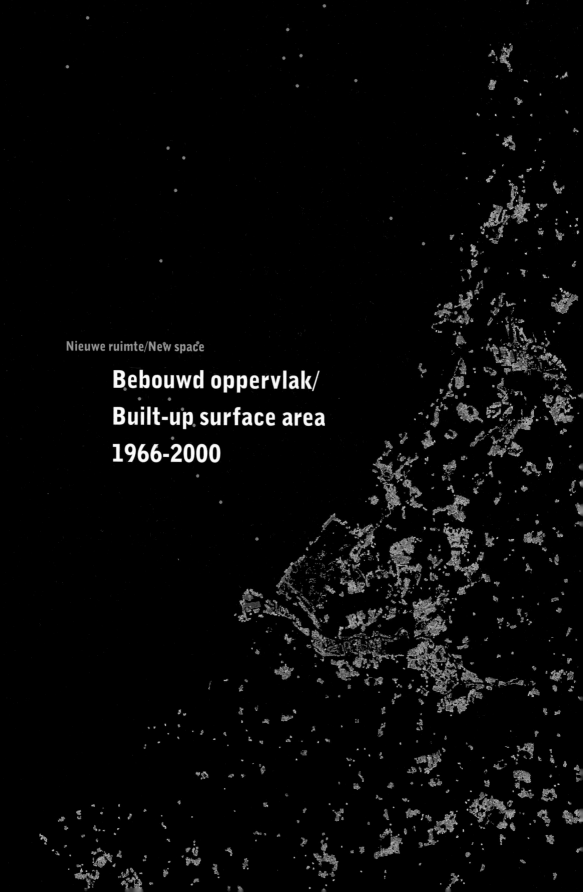

Nieuwe ruimte/New space

Bebouwd oppervlak/ Built-up surface area 1966-2000

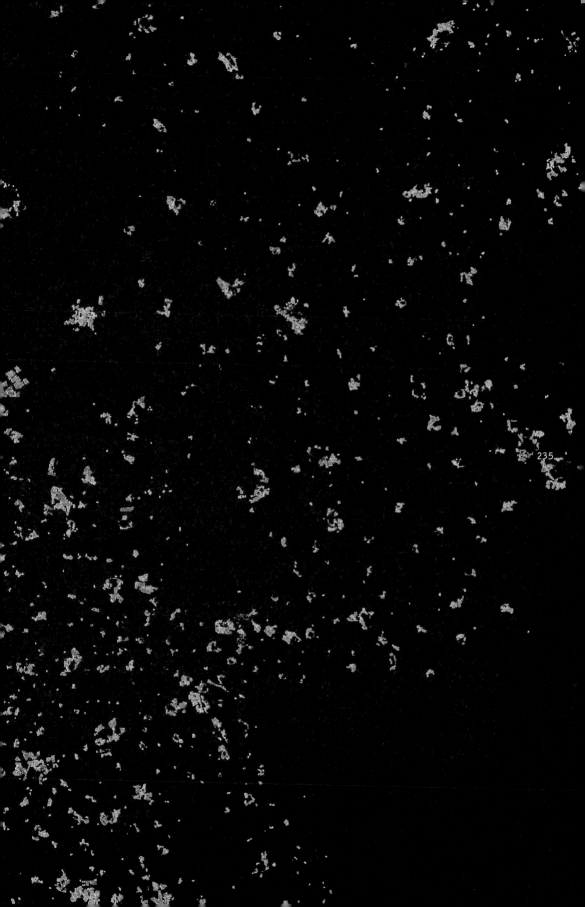
235

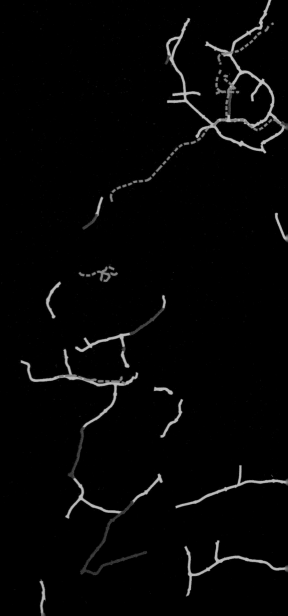

Nieuwe ruimte/New space

Infrastructuur/
Infrastructure
1966-2000

Nieuwe ruimte/New space

Afname openheid/
Reduction of the openness
1966-2000

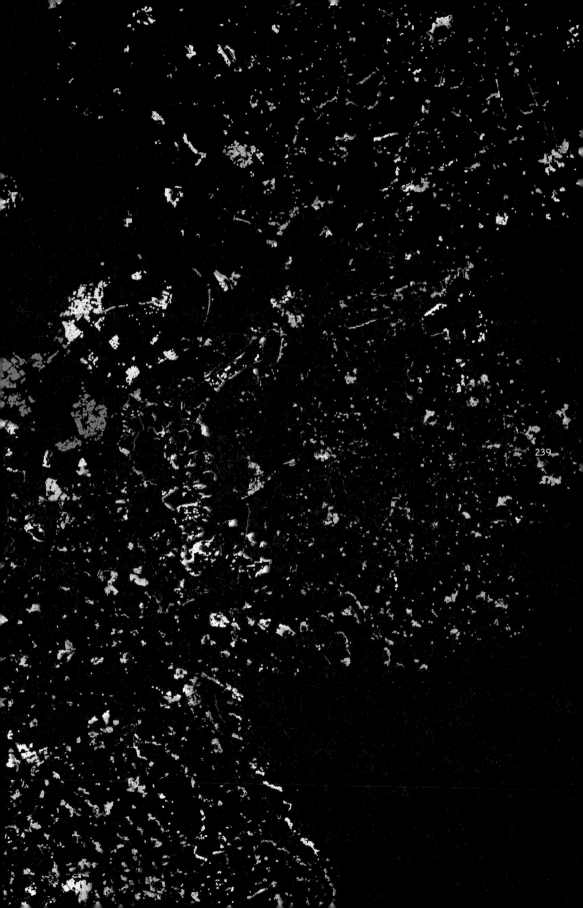

New usage forms

Metabolism, the continuous extraction, transportation and disposal of raw materials. Where do we drill for gas and oil and where do we extract construction materials, how are these transported, what do we need them for, and where do they end up as waste?

The **recreational landscape**. Where do people play? Where are the most important recreation areas, amusement parks and national parks? Which recreational routes are we advised to take, and which landscapes do we find attractive?

Gasfield		Residential location		Scenic route (Michelin)	
Sand quarrying		Urban field		○ Important sight	
· Other quarrying/ mineral extraction		Rubbish tip		• Recreation park	
• Platform		· Cemetery		• Amusement park	
● Power station		· Wrecking yard		➤ Bungalow park	
⌣ 60-bar gas main				• Golf course	
⌢ 40-bar gas main				• Zoo	
⌢ Oil and other pipelines				• Children's playground	
⌣ High-voltage pylons/cable				• Theme park	

How accessible is the Netherlands? Which places are open to the public, where are there selective admission policies, which areas are you only allowed to enter with a valid membership card or admission ticket and which areas are private and inaccessible?

Allotments	Airport	Zoo
Sports facility	Military zone – land	Theme park
Park	Military zone – sea	Motorway
Overnight recreation	Nature reserve	Railway
Other day-trip recreation	Golf course	Public access
Woodland	Amusement park	Restricted access
Sandbars	Bungalow park	
Fresh water	Recreation park	
Salt water	Children's playground	

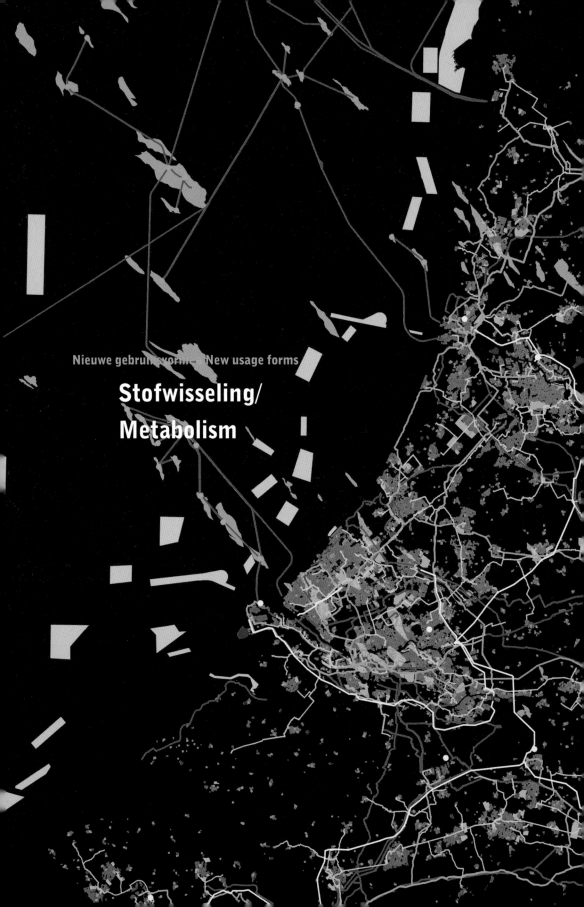

Nieuwe gebruiksvormen/New usage forms

Stofwisseling/
Metabolism

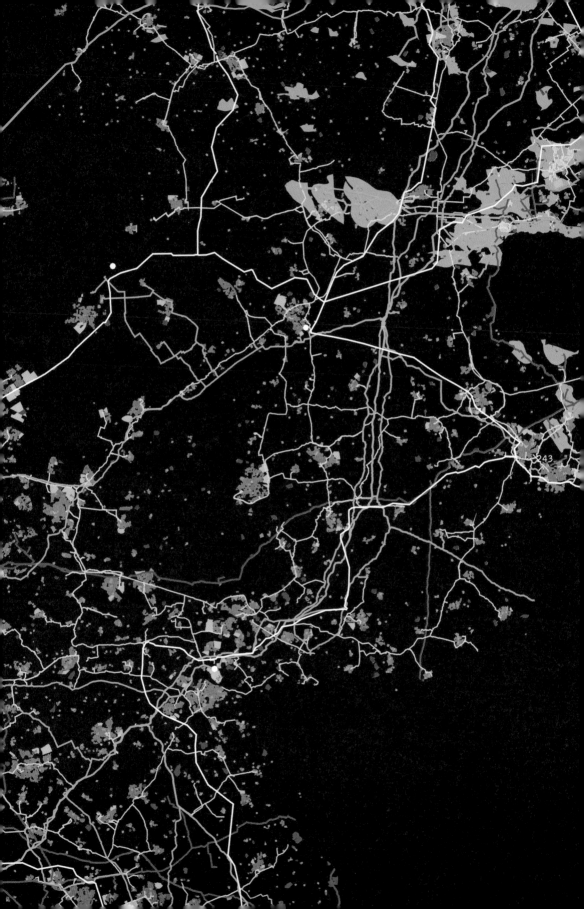

Nieuwe gebruiksvormen/New usage forms

Recreatief landschap/
Recreational landscape

Nieuwe gebruiksvormen/New usage forms

Toegankelijkheid/
Accessibility

Judith van der Laan, IT consultant, flies all round the globe on business. Her Dutch operating base in the Netherlands is in Beilen, in the middle of the natural beauty of the province of Drenthe. She spends most of her precious free time as a volunteer for Natuurmonumenten, the Dutch nature conservation organization.

Henk de Bruin, a salesman of coffee machines, crisscrosses from one end of the Netherlands to the other every day in his leased van. Zwolle Zuid is the centre of his life. This is where his friends and family live, where he finds his day-to-day conveniences, and his favourite Sunday stroll.

Mies de Jong, a retired beauty specialist, spends most of the year in sunny Sitges on the Mediterranean Sea. She regularly takes the high-speed train to visit her apartment on the ring of canals in Amsterdam's historic centre. Her most important activity in the Netherlands is visiting her three children.

Chicago

Nieuwe gebruikers/New users

Judith van der Laan

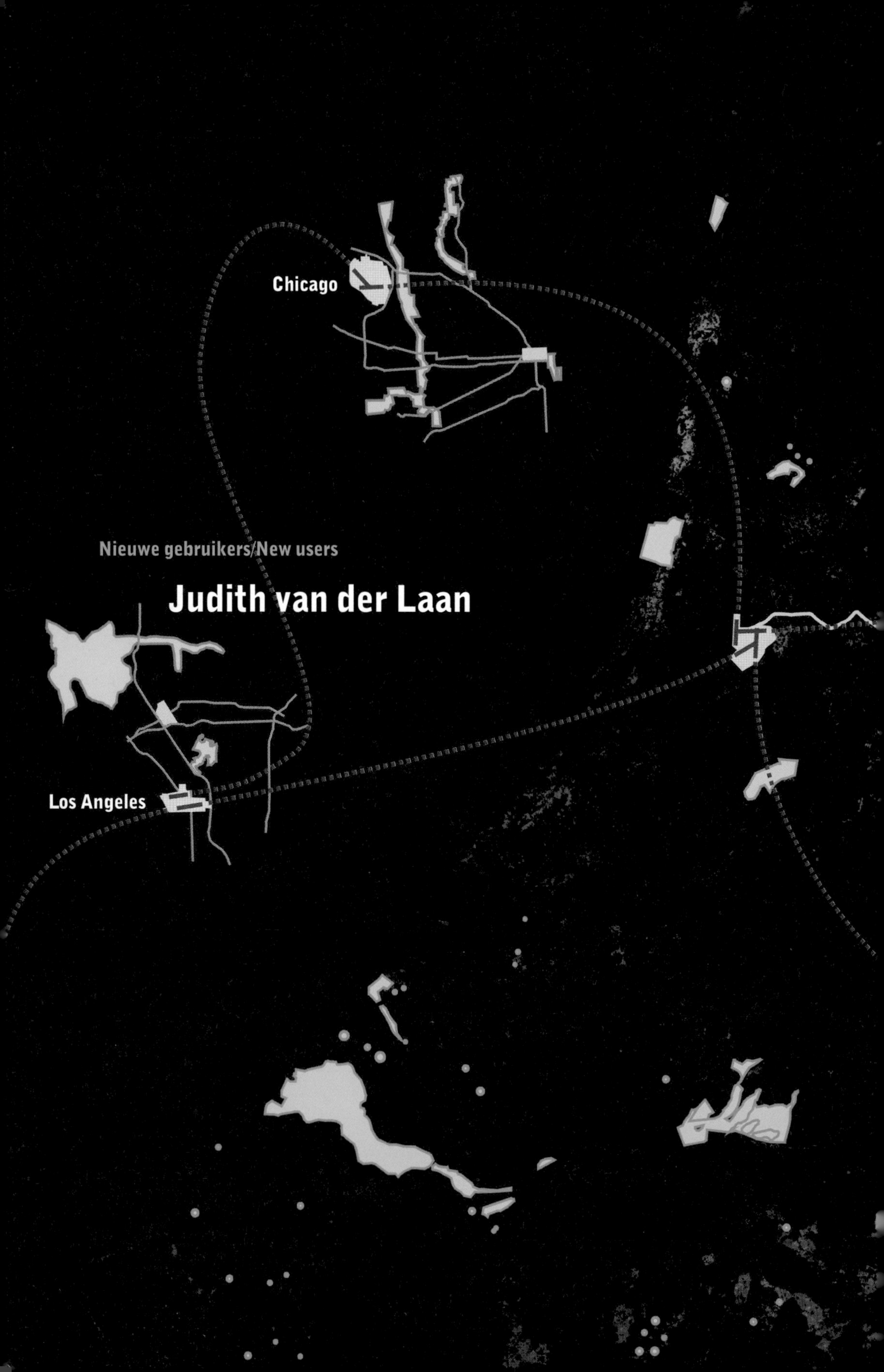

Los Angeles

Beilen

Osaka

251

Singapore

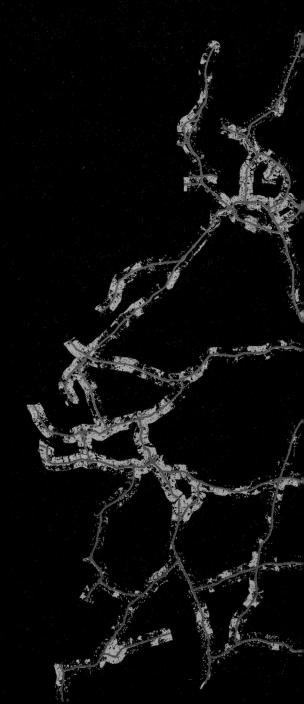

Nieuwe gebruikers/New users

Henk de Bruin

Scheppinckmate 16a
Zwolle Zuid

253

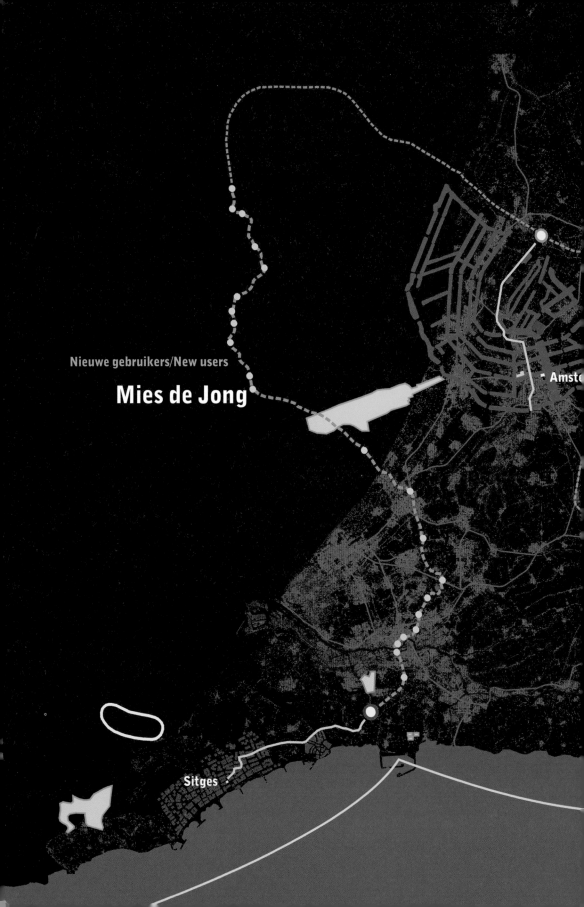

Nieuwe gebruikers/New users

Mies de Jong

Amste

Sitges

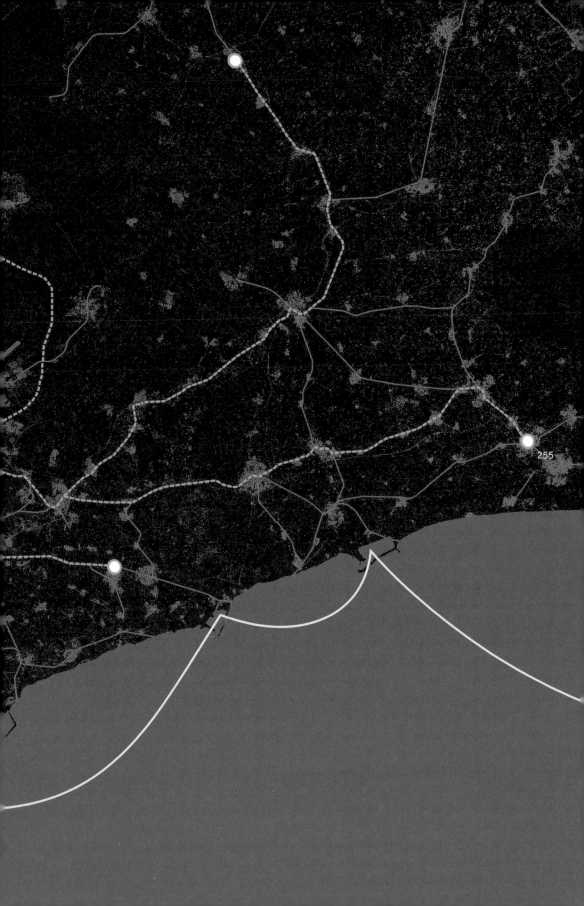

Contributions

Theo Baart has published the photographic volumes Hollandse Interieurs (1994), Snelweg › Highways in the Netherlands (1996) (in collaboration with Cary Markerink) and Bouwlust (1999).

Tracy Metz, born in the United States of America, works as an editor for NRC Handelsblad newspaper, for which she writes on architecture, urban planning and landscape. She wrote Nieuwe Natuur: Reportages over veranderend landschap (1998) and coedited Snelweg › Highways in the Netherlands.

Tjerk Ruimschotel is an urban planning expert and advises the municipality of Almere, among others. He was one of the initiators of De Nieuwe Kaart van Nederland (1997).

Must is a laboratory for urban design and research. It establishes collaborative relations tailored to the specific requirements of a project, on every level from local to European. The laboratory's permanent home is in Amsterdam, but its mobile workstation criss-crosses Europe.

Typography & Other Serious Matters is a typographic design bureau. Their work includes SubUrban Options (1998), Snelweg › Highways in the Netherlands (1996) and Bouwlust (1999).

The Ideas on Paper foundation is active in the fields of photography and design. Previous projects include Snelweg › Highways in the Netherlands (1996) and Bouwlust (1999).

Acknowledgements photography

Big Spotters Hill, Floriade – Haarlemmermeer, Niek Roozen. Borg Wolveschans – Leek, Charles Vandenhove. Leisure Park – Enschede, Engineers'/Architects' Association. Erasmus Bridge – Rotterdam, UN Studio / Ben van Berkel & Caroline Bos. Renovation of postwar neighbourhoods – Geinwijk/Gerenstein, Amsterdam Zuid-Oost, Ton Venhoeven, Claus & Kaan, Geurst & Schulze. Wadi Ruwenbos, Vinex site, Eschmarke – Enschede, Buildings and Environment Services, Enschede Municipal Council; Project designers Leijh Kappelhoff Seckel; Kristinsson; Inbo & NIBAG.

Sources

Bouw, periodical for architecture and construction, Blauwe Kamer, periodical for landscape development and urban planing, Incoldelta workgroup on land-use quality, NRC Handelsblad newspaper, McArthurGlen press release, Designers Outlet, 'Ruimtelijke Verkenningen' 1998 and 1999, Trouw newspaper, de Volkskrant newspaper, Belvédère Beleidsnota over de relatie cultuur-historie en ruimtelijke inrichting (1999), De Ruimte van Nederland: Startnota ruimtelijke ordening 1999.

Maps

Fragment from De Nieuwe Kaart van Nederland (NIROV, The Hague), 1997 edition. The map provides an overview of the plans and projects to be realized through 2005.
'4 Perspectieven 2030' from Nederland 2030 – Discussienota, Verkenningen Ruimtelijke Perspectieven (VROM, Ministry of Housing, Spatial Planning and the Environment, The Hague, 1997).
'Structuurbeeld van Nederland in ruimere omgeving' from the 2e Nota Ruimtelijke Ordening (1966).
'Ruimtelijke structuurschets voor Nederland omstreeks 2000' from the 2e Nota Ruimtelijke Ordening (1966).